T0356708

# I'll Look So Hot
## in a Coffin

# I'll Look So Hot in a Coffin

## And Other Thoughts I Used to Have About My Body

Carla Sosenko

THE DIAL PRESS

NEW YORK

The Dial Press
An imprint of Random House
A division of Penguin Random House LLC
1745 Broadway, New York, NY 10019
randomhousebooks.com
penguinrandomhouse.com

Portions of Chapter 5 appeared in different form in "How I Learned That Food—Unlike Morality—Doesn't Have a Positive or Negative Charge" (PULP, November 18, 2019). Portions of Chapter 1 and Chapter 10 originally appeared in different form in "Getting a Tattoo Affirmed That My Body Is a Dictatorship, Not a Democracy—and I'm the HBIC" (Well & Good, May 9, 2019).

Hardcover ISBN 978-0-593-59589-3
Ebook ISBN 978-0-593-59590-9

Printed in the United States of America on acid-free paper

1st Printing

First Edition

BOOK TEAM: Production editor: Jennifer Rodriguez • Managing editor: Rebecca Berlant • Production manager: Jennifer Backe • Copy editor: Caroline Clouse • Proofreaders: Melissa Churchill, Amy Harned, Emily Zebrowski

*Book design by Sara Bereta*

The authorized representative in the EU for product safety and compliance is Penguin Random House Ireland, Morrison Chambers, 32 Nassau Street, Dublin D02 YH68, Ireland. https://eu-contact.penguin.ie

For M+D

The author has taken narrative liberties
in order to protect the privacy of jerks.

# Contents

# I'll Look So Hot in a Coffin

# Preface.

## *One Day I'll Look Like Everyone Else!*

*O*nce *I'm dead, I'll have a symmetrical tush, legs that match, and a flat back; I'll be so thin, I'll be skeletal.* This is something I used to tell myself whenever my quest to change or shrink my deformed body was failing, which was often. *One day, in a coffin, I'll look like everyone else.*

I was born with the congenital vascular disorder Klippel-Trenaunay syndrome, named for the French doctors who discovered it.* K-T affects anywhere from one to five in every

---

* There is a chance, I have learned in adulthood, based on my particular abnormalities, that what I actually have is CLOVES syndrome, which was sometimes mistaken for K-T around the time of my birth in the 1970s. CLOVES stands for congenital lipomatous overgrowth, vascular malformations, epidermal nevi, and scoliosis/skeletal/spinal anomalies (rolls off the tongue, doesn't it?). I have never cared enough about naming my de-

100,000 people and is unique to every person who has it; it can be a disability or even a life threatener for some, not for others. I'm one of the lucky ones, but I do live in a body that is significantly, visibly different from most. There is a hypertrophy of tissue on my back, rendering it giant, blobby, lopsided, and not very back-like. My torso, right leg, and bottom are marked by soft, uneven malformations and a port wine stain so big it looks like a spilled bottle of sun-faded cabernet.

These idiosyncrasies beget others: tilted posture, jutting cervical spine, anemia, probably—no doctor I've talked to has been able to conclusively prove the connection, but everyone I've met with K-T is iron deficient.

I got my varicose veins embolized in my thirties, and the doctor, who has lots of patients with K-T, said about my insides afterward, "We saw some crazy anatomy in there, even by *our* standards!" More recently, a hiatal hernia required surgery that revealed more things I'd never known: My organs were squished. My stomach was up in my chest. Nothing was quite where it should be.

Depending on my angles and the viewer's narcissism, some people meet me and never notice the deformity. Others think I'm pregnant. Others think I'm fat, which I also am, though not all parts of me are (my left leg is thin and muscular, my fingers are long and bony), and my weight fluctuates as much as is in-

---

formity to find out whether my diagnosis is accurate, and I've been lucky enough (toi, toi, toi) that I've never needed to, though I will admit that "CLOVES" has a slightly nicer ring to it than the hideous-sounding "Klippel" and "Trénaunay" (*désolée, docteurs!*).

evitable for anyone who has spent her whole life trying to control it. Some people look at me and then ask questions that seem like non sequiturs—Are you a dancer? Are you an athlete?—I guess because they're trying, in real time, to process a body they can't make sense of. Some just squish up their faces in confusion (been *there*, babe).

When I'm naked, from certain angles I look sort of like a purple yam, but one of the misfits people discard in favor of more symmetrical tubers. I always grab the weirdos when I'm grocery shopping, out of solidarity.

My face, I have been told since I was little, is pretty. Whether it is or isn't is, of course, subjective and also doesn't really matter (sometimes I like it, sometimes I don't) except in the way it split me in two very early on. My face was good and my body was bad. Some people have told me I am the prettiest person they have ever seen; others have insinuated that I am so opposite of pretty, I do not deserve to live. I'm sure many people think I am forgettable and average, if "average" is meant to mean "nothing special" and not what it actually means.

I have sometimes felt like all of these things simultaneously, which is as much of a mindfuck as it sounds like. For a long time, when I was told I had a pretty face I took it to be a compliment, but an asterisked one, a pity, because *look at the rest of me.* "Such a pretty face," said with a rueful shake of the head and a tsk-tsk. What a waste, what a loss. I viewed myself in pieces, which isn't really the way to view a self, especially when it's your own.

I was shockingly innocent about my body for a very long time because I spent most of my life avoiding it. The best way I

5

can describe my relationship to my back, for example, is that I would recognize it in a lineup but could not accurately describe it for a sketch artist. Could you describe yours? I don't know how well a person is supposed to know her back.

When I was forced to look at my body—when others compelled me to—I knew neither what to make of it nor what possibility it held. I had spent so much time thinking that maybe, yes, once my insides were worm food, the remaining bits of bone would look like everyone else's. But eventually, thank god, a more important question crossed my mind: *What's so great about looking like everyone else, especially when you're dead?*

I no longer care what people experience when they look at me. I care only what *I* experience, and what I experience is gratitude. Today, I realize that my body is just my body, nothing more and nothing less. I recognize that it is not perfect and it is not flawless and that "perfect" and "flawless" are social constructs that are slowly but surely disintegrating as fat bodies and differently abled bodies and otherwise marginalized bodies increasingly refuse to be sidelined or pressured to change or stopped from changing if change is what makes a particular body feel right. Most important, most days, I am able to remember that this is the only body I've got, take it or leave it, and it is a monumental waste of time to spend one more minute hating myself, especially when there are so many other people willing (and happy!) to do that for me.

I don't want to make it sound easy, because it isn't and wasn't. First came a decision to want to find happiness, then therapy as a geolocation tool. That took a long time. Then antidepressants. More therapy. Age, which is the hands-down best antidote to giving a fuck. It was all hard—but hard is not impossible.

I believe we are on the cusp of a movement to uplift the multitudes of us who live in unique bodies, who've perhaps felt allyship with disabled and trans and fat-liberation communities but have never had a place of our own. I hope this book can be a part of it. I hope it can even inspire and enlighten people with bodies that are technically, by society's standards, "normal"; who may be unintentionally and unwittingly benefitting from the marginalization of others but who have also likely had their own moments of feeling not good enough, because the world is nothing if not hard on people and especially hard on women.

Some of us fall into multiple camps. Yes, I am deformed, but I am also a small fat, cishet woman with pretty privilege. I am a fair-skinned Jew, which means I benefit from white privilege while white nationalists chant, "Jews will not replace us" and bigots who share no other common ground with neo-Nazis cheer them on.

I have been fortunate in ways that people in other marginalized communities, and even some in the K-T community, have not. I have been an outsider and an insider simultaneously. Sometimes I've thought the only consistent thing about me is my not fitting in anywhere perfectly. But a lot of people think that about themselves, and if enough of us feel like outsiders, doesn't that sort of make us the insiders?

It's all been really confusing.

I call my body unconventional because I have not yet

thought of a better word. It's a placeholder. As conventions change—as we change them—so will my adjective.

This is one story, mine, of a lived experience: the way I sometimes feel unsafe moving through the world; the way fatness and my disorder have been conflated and confused; the way dating has been hard for me; the way my view of myself has been both undermined and propped up by my love of fashion; the way my body has felt like public property sometimes, with people perfectly comfortable asking me questions about it or even touching it, as if I have given them permission simply by existing.

This is also a story about what it means to be sick or spent—or defiantly insistent that you're not—in a culture that rewards overwork and that glossy sheen of burnout, and a world that prizes thinness above all else, including mental health, which can wither in its pursuit. Throughout my life, I have been told—and told myself—to pull myself up by my unevenly worn bootstraps and push myself and soldier on and muscle through and diet, diet, diet. It has all been a way of making myself feel normal. I have equated a lack of energy with a lack of drive, motivation, and ambition and rallied against the instinct to rest even when it's meant I can barely lift myself out of bed. Anytime I have felt the ultimate shame of laziness, I have blamed myself instead of empathically understanding that there is a constellation of valid reasons for my exhaustion and also that all reasons are valid when one needs—or wants—to just sit down and stop for a while.

I have generalized anxiety disorder. I have S-curve scoliosis.

I have (I learned very late, like a lot of women) ADHD. I have two legs that are not the same weight or length and therefore make walking different for me than for other people. I have flat feet and bad rotator cuffs. For a long time, none of those things mattered when it came to self-compassion—they seemed like copouts and excuses—but I am working on that and finally being kinder to myself, wondering instead, *Why* wouldn't *I be tired?* Why wouldn't walking around in this body take an effort? Why wouldn't just existing in this world, no matter what your body is like, knock the wind out of you sometimes?

At forty-seven, I hurt in ways I didn't used to. When the movie *Everything Everywhere All at Once* came out, I thought that might make a nice title for a list of my body parts that ache and when. Some of it is age. Some of it is my size. I hesitate to say that—fatness does not equal out-of-shapeness—but this is part of my deprogramming, too. I do not need to stack up to thin people. I do not need to prove that I am capable of doing everything they can. I do not owe them that. I need to do the much harder job of persuading people that those of us who are fat or deformed or disabled or all of the above need not do everything our thin, "conventional" peers do in order to deserve dignity and respect.

I want people who have felt left out or isolated or "one of a kind" in a way that feels synonymous with "alone" or "wrong" or "inadequate" to read my book and think, *FUCK YES, THIS,* because the power of allyship and understanding goes a very long way. I'm pretty sure it saved my life.

I want those who have felt a sort of safety in flittering at the margins and hydroplaning on the surface to feel able and deserving of plunging their grubby little mitts into life and eating up every last bit of it.

I want us to demand to be seen. Right now, when I watch TV and films, or flip through magazines, I think, *Where the hell are we?* Where is the alopecia? Where are the cleft palates? Where are the infinifats? Where is the Klippel-Trenaunay? (One in 100,000 may be a small number, but that number isn't zero.) And while we're at it, where are all of us in a way that doesn't focus solely on the thing that makes us supposedly different, that isn't sensationalized, that isn't about how our specific thing equals our entire specific story? Others may want to make our difference all of it, make it take up 100 percent of our lives 100 percent of the time, but that's simply not real.

Representation is improving (shows and films out of the UK and Ireland seem to do a particularly good job), but it needs to go faster. I want us to be seen, and in order to be seen, we need to be shown going about our lives, the way we do, because we are people. (Producers, call me.)

I want to see humans like me on runways and covers. Hell, I want to see *me* on runways and covers. (Designers and editors, call me.)

I want other people who have ever felt that their bodies must be hidden or asterisked or apologized for or *shrunken erased depleted deleted* to know that they do not. I want them to feel that it is not only okay to be proud of their bodies, it is fucking punk rock.

There is safety in numbers. There is comfort in common

experience, even when the only thing our experiences have in common is how unique they are.


I am finally proud of my body—and of me—deformity and all. Not every day. Not every second. But most of the time, yeah.

As a writer, I make sense of the world with words. I'm going to tell you how I made sense—how I am still making sense—of mine. It was a long road to get here (and a scattershot one, so strap in). (I hope you like digressions!) (And parentheses!) (I mentioned the ADHD, right?) I have detoured and doubled back, and sometimes I regress, but never permanently. My journey has not been—will not be—flawless. I'm hoping the things I've learned can give you a shortcut on your own path, or even just the inkling of one. I don't have all the answers and I am still learning, but I hope that's reassuring, too, in its own way.

# 1.

## It's Okay to Let the Bastards Get You Down, Just Get Back Up When You Can (They Hate That)

There have been so many bastards, I could start practically anywhere. But there is one standout. A bastard to end all bastards. We crossed paths when I was twenty-eight.

It was at a bar in Chelsea, where someone who knew someone who knew someone was having a combo birthday-Halloween party. My look was thrown together because I'd been planning to stay home, but at the last minute, my friend Annie persuaded me to go.

As an adult, I've never been a huge fan of Halloween. Putting on a costume instead of an outfit I love does not excite me, nor does gallivanting with an entire city that is drunk and high and inhibition-free. When the invitation materialized, I put on an all-black outfit and dug out a headband with devil horns that I for some reason owned and figured it would have to do.

I noticed a man across the bar who looked familiar. He was

dressed like a vampire in a halfhearted way: fangs, fake blood around the mouth, a cape.

If this had happened in the more recent past, his costume would seem too on the nose for my story. In the era of *Twilight* and Lisa Taddeo and Olivia Rodrigo, my using a vampire would be cliché and derivative. But this really was the costume he chose, not one I am giving him as a fictional flourish. Maybe the universe was trying to warn me.

I am someone who is terrible with names but gifted when it comes to remembering faces. If I sit next to you on the subway today and pass you on the street four years from now, it may take a minute, but I'll eventually remember why you look familiar. As soon as I saw the vampire, I knew: He had been at Club Med recently, the same time I was there with Annie. Though I didn't remember anything specifically good about him that made me want to reconnect, my outgoingness prevailed that night, and I ran over to him, explaining that we'd been in Turks and Caicos at the same time.

Club Med was the first adultish vacation I'd ever taken, and Annie and I loved it, even though it forced us into social situations when maybe we didn't want to be, like at meals. The vampire had been at our table at least once, and by the end of our trip, we'd seen him strutting around the pool with the resort's current Queen Bee, a skinny blond with big tits.

On Halloween, the vampire and I drifted apart and together and apart again, talking about mostly nothing. He complained that Queen Bee had become sort of obsessed with him, wanting to visit him in New York, and didn't she realize it was just a vacation thing? I spent a lot of time talking to a dancer who took my phone number and made me swear to come see him in the *Christmas Spectacular,* which we both knew I wouldn't do. Bar promises, lies we tell each other, it was all part of the fun. The room was crowded and sticky and loud; just your average extraordinary night in New York.

Then I heard, "Hey, Carla. C'mere."

It was the vampire, sitting at the bar with two people, a girl and a guy I hadn't noticed earlier. Though I didn't know them, they felt familiar; they had the vague look of the spoiled, boring kids I grew up with on Long Island turned Midtown East day traders. They were the type of people who have never interested me but whose approval I long sought anyway.

I obeyed the vampire's command and found myself standing in front of him and his friends.

"What's up?" I said.

"What's on your back?" he asked.

I swear I knew it was coming. Something in his eyes, maybe. An unkind little hint. I don't know when he noticed my body. Long enough before asking that he had time to cook up a plan. Somewhere between my eagerly, stupidly seeking him out at the start of the night and this very moment.

Now, facing the vampire's question, his entourage of enablers waiting for me to answer, I responded: "Do you really want to know, or are you being a jerk?"

"I don't think he's being a jerk," his male friend offered.

"I wasn't asking you," I said.

"I am really asking what's on your back," the vampire told me, a smirk creeping onto his face. "I genuinely want to know."

"It's a congenital disorder I was born with," I replied, thinking to myself as I spoke, *Congenital* means *"born with," you idiot.* I don't know why I kept answering him, but I couldn't stop myself. It was as if I thought compliance would get me out of the pickle I'd found myself in. No, that's wrong. It wasn't a pickle and I hadn't found myself there. It was a minefield, and I'd ignored the warning signs—DANGER! DO NOT ENTER!— and tromped right in.

The vampire's smirk was stuck now—he was ready for his finale. It felt like hours had passed.

"Turn around so I can *feel* it," he ordered me. He wanted to feel my back. He wanted to touch it with his hands. His voice never wavered. He was calm; he seemed very happy with himself.

That finally unstuck me from my place; I was too proud to let this motherfucker put his hands on me, though I would later play out a version in which I did: I'd turn around and let him touch my back. He'd laugh, sharing whispers with his friends, who would also reach out to cop a feel, my implicit permission granted because if I let the vampire, why shouldn't they all get a turn? With every touch I'd disintegrate just a little bit more, a human Shrinky Dink activated by their hot, greedy hands.

There's another scenario I later imagined, too, one that entailed revenge and righteous comeuppance, some gathering of superhero-like strength that unleashed itself in a violent fit that made all three Borings sorry they'd started with me. Or something quieter, like my calmly picking up one of the candles on the bar and holding it near the girl's hair, setting her ablaze. If I could get only one of them, it would have to be her; the betrayal of sisterhood was so immense, she'd have to bear the brunt of it. Another woman paying for the transgressions of men.

Outside, not quite sure how I got there, I began to hyperventilate. Annie suddenly materialized and I told her what had happened, or tried to, because there was no adequate way to explain it. I didn't know how to describe tonight without making it feel bigger or smaller than it was. What *did* happen? A not-so-nice man said not-so-nice things about the fact that my body looked different than other people's, something I knew and had known my whole life?

It bothered me that I couldn't remember his name. It bothered me more that I was just a quick diversion, a bit of fun to be had in a night that must have bored him otherwise, because as I was standing in the street, finally getting my breath back, I saw him leave with his friends.

Annie tried to convince me to stay and offered to go home with me when I refused, but I said no. And so I walked. I was drunk and tired and crying, but so were a lot of people. I was just another crying girl in the city on Halloween. My feet hurt, and I was limping by the time I found a cab three avenues away, tights torn, makeup running.

When I was finally in my bed, I was crying still and not sure I'd be able to stop. A tap that had been rumbling for a long time was now open. *A one-in-100,000 chance, the only lottery I'd ever won. Why? Why did I get this body?* It was something I'd always wondered. The roll of the dice. The flip of a coin. Just my luck.

I didn't waste my time with other questions—*Why did he target me? What did I ever do to him?*—because the answers didn't matter. Instead, for the first time in my life, I fantasized about being beaten to a bloody pulp. My mind went there easily. I thought about offering someone money to assault me, assuring them it was okay because I deserved it. I pictured myself bruised, swollen, bloody, broken, in a hospital bed, practically unrecognizable, my friends and family gazing down at my tortured body—my poor, poor body—shaking their heads and weeping.

I had never done anything remotely like this—I still don't know where the idea came from—but I was instantly enthralled, addicted to the imagined feeling of being hurt. Elated by it. Comforted. And finally I fell asleep, no longer crying, calm.

Every night after, for years, this was my ritual. I would crawl into bed and, regardless of the mood I was in before, start to cry and fantasize about being hurt. Some people counted sheep. I lulled myself to sleep with explicit visions of being brutalized. I had never cut myself, but my practice made me understand the feeling cutters describe, how it's a release. How the physical pain—even the idea of it—was a salve. I never died in my fantasies, I only came close. There was no fun in disappearing completely; I needed to make others look at what I had endured because I thought I deserved it.

Here's the stranger part: Years before, in that same bed, there was a specific moment in which I thought, *You don't actually hate your body now, but you will.* It felt like it came out of nowhere. It couldn't have been true, because what sort of person knows they *will* hate their body if they don't already, at least a little? I must have sensed that some people detested me so much for my difference, I would eventually have no choice but to join them. I was either preparing myself or trying to ward off the inevitable with magical thinking. Maybe I was just observant. I saw how much this world values beauty, and not just any kind—not the *jolie laide* or the differently abled—but the thin, white, big-titted, curves-in-only-the-right-places Club Med kind, so maybe I was trying to ready myself for when I would join their ranks.

I had experienced teen angst like everybody else, but it always felt performative, even when I would make broody scrawls of the word "freak" on a slip of paper, with all the letters different sizes, like the pieces of my body. I felt more ordinary than anything else.

I wondered why the vampire was the one who finally wrecked me, who tipped me over that edge. When I told my therapist, Marilyn, about him the week after Halloween, she suggested it was my own state of denial that set me up so perfectly to be toppled. I had been living in a sort of

re-creation of a
1995 self-portrait

bubble, disconnected from my body and the reality of it—kneecapped by years of dieting, exhausted from so much pointless dating, weak and easy to prey on—so that when the vampire attacked, it was like being awakened from a dream, and the result was catastrophic. There was nothing inherently special about him other than the straightforwardness of his cruelty.

Others had obviously broken the spell before. I'd be going

about my business, feeling like a normal person, virtually forgetting that I wasn't one, and someone would touch me or shoot me a quizzical look or just ask, and the spell would falter: I'm not normal, I haven't fooled anyone. Afterward I would sulk or wallow or collapse in on myself. I'd get knocked down, but I'd get up again (you're never gonna keep me down). The guy on Halloween did more long-lasting damage because he happened to strike at a time when I was—without realizing it—particularly vulnerable to vampires and bastards.

## 2.

---

## *If You See Something, Say Nothing*

---

f you are a human being, chances are people have commented on your looks at some point. If you're a woman, this is 99.9 percent more likely to be true. If you are a woman who is not white or a woman who is not cis or a woman with a body that is different from the kinds of bodies people are used to and therefore comfortable with, that percentage soars to a whopping 100.* Keep in mind that "used to" and "comfortable with" can change from place to place and depending on who's looking. If you are in the United States like I am, the lens is one that, when it comes to women, usually sees thin, able-bodied, not deformed cis white femmes the most clearly; everyone else is slightly out of focus, and people feel an intrinsic right to ask questions

---

\* I made up these numbers but would bet my life that they are accurate or on the low side.

about the things that aren't clear to them. That's the price you pay for being blurry, even though so many of us are. On that note, here:

## An Incomplete List, in No Particular Order, of Things People Have Said to Me About My Body

---

### "At least it didn't hit your face." —An allergist

---

I was thirty-seven, and I'd never seen this doctor before. I was visiting her because during a brief delusion, I considered letting a boyfriend move into my apartment with his cat, even though cats turn me into a puffy splotch. The doctor had never heard of Klippel-Trenaunay. Once I explained it, her assessment was a look-on-the-bright-side kind of affirmation that this rare syndrome had messed up my body but thank god not my face. I dumped the allergist but not the boyfriend (which was a mistake; more on that later).

---

### "You have too much fat on your thigh." —My kindergarten music teacher

---

Our class was getting ready for a recital, and Mrs. Trindadi had decided to add a dance routine. She asked who among us had a leotard at home, and my hand sailed up of its own accord; I took jazz, ballet, and tap at Arlene & Cathy's School of Dance like most of the girls. But no, my right thigh was not thin enough for her production, said Mrs. Trindadi, and so my navy zip-up leotard stayed home for the recital, and I sang but did not dance.

---

> "Are you crying because you can't
> wear a T-shirt in the pool?" —The director
> of Pitch Pine Woods sleepaway camp

---

It was 1989 and I was twelve years old; it was my first summer away from home. I'd been cautiously optimistic at the prospect of camp. I knew a lot of people who went to sleepaway and loved it, so I wanted to try. Upon my arrival, I stepped off the bus, inhaled the thick, wet scent of Catskills grass, and immediately burst into tears. It came upon me without warning, this terrible overwhelmingness in my body—a shaking, then the feeling that nothing would ever be good again. I found my way to Bunk 10 and located the most adult-looking person in the room, a counselor who was probably eighteen.

"Hi," I said. "Can you take me to talk to someone, please? I'd like to go home."

When your parents are paying four thousand dollars for a summer of go-karting, candle-making, and Color War, it stands to reason that if you no longer want to enjoy any of those things, you can simply change your mind. Not so, I learned. Elena, the counselor, walked me to the main house and deposited me in front of Camp Director Marge Cohn, a chain-smoking math teacher, and I told her, through hiccups and sobs, that I wanted to leave.

"You need to give it some time," she said, expressionless. "You just got here."

*Exactly,* I thought: I just got here and already my body is rebelling, doing things it never has before, so clearly camp was a mistake. Could I please talk to my parents?

The answer was a definitive no. Talking to my parents would only make things worse, Marge said, though I couldn't imagine what "worse" would feel like. I was sent to unpack my three extra-large duffel bags and get straight to the business of giving it time. The next morning and most succeeding ones that first week, I woke up and immediately started hyperventilating. Sometimes I woke up to find myself already crying, a horrifying new talent.

Had there been a child psychologist on staff, she might have explained anxiety and its predictability, told me that it's typically at its worst in the morning and that the best thing to do, counterintuitive as it may sound, is to get yourself out of bed and into a shower. Maybe she would have taught me breathwork or yoga. Maybe she could have convinced me that things *do* take time and if I could just hang in there, everything really would get better.

But Pitch Pine was a tough-love camp, and my constant crying was deemed a challenge for me to overcome. Like learning to macramé or tie-dye, I'd have to figure out a way through this particular item—shorthanded as "homesickness"—on my summer to-do list.

Time slows down in camp, and that first week felt endless. I wrote letters to my parents every day, usually on "I Love Camp" stationery, though I'd cross out "Love" and replace it with "Hate." My critical mistake was doing this on both the inside and the envelope, which meant, I eventually learned, that some of my letters got no farther than Marge's desk.

Counselors were dispatched in shifts to babysit me—some with attitude (Lou, you were tough but cool), others with affection (thank you forever, Kate and Helen), the worst with casual indifference (fuck you, Elena), and even though I insisted to all of them that I hated it there just as much as I had that very first day, I *did* sense the nervousness releasing its grip just a little. I was making friends. I was playing sports. I had my River Phoenix posters arranged exactly as I wanted them on the wall behind my bed. By evening canteen most nights, I was happily playing ping-pong with boys I found cute—the two objects of my affection had similarly ridiculous names: Blake Brossman and Bryson Block—though even in my best moments I still had the faintest glimmer of panic in the pit of my stomach, taunting me with its imminent return to full strength. "See you tomorrow morning," it would say. "Don't get too big for your britches."

The crying would not cease. The counselors were tiring of me, I could tell. I was demanding too much of their attention. Unlike most camps, which are eight weeks, Pitch Pine was four—that's why my parents and I had chosen it—and a full quarter of the summer was already nearly gone.

So there I was, sitting at Marge's desk again for what was starting to feel like a standing appointment. She must have been at the end of her rope, because she finally asked what I guess she'd been wondering the whole time: "Are you crying because you can't wear a T-shirt in the pool?"

Her question confounded me. Yes, I was homesick, we all agreed, but I didn't understand what swimming—and the camp's safety ban on T-shirts over bathing suits—had to do with anything. It was as if she'd asked whether I knew that two plus two equaled molasses. Not only did I not care about the T-shirt rule, but in that first week of camp—when I could stop crying long enough to get into the pool or just swam with tears streaming down my face, because who could tell the difference—it was clear that I had one of the best backstrokes in the division. My freestyle had even beaten David Zimmerman's during a relay with boys camp. I'd shown no signs of shame as I stood on the edge of the pool in my red racing suit waiting to jump in, nor when I climbed out to get on the diving board line, because I felt none. I was a water baby; there are few places that make me as calm and happy as pools and oceans. I hadn't ever asked to wear a T-shirt while I swam.

Yet it was the only explanation Marge could fathom—that my unhappiness must have to do with my body. Her question lodged somewhere deep, its implication clear: If she were me, she'd want to wear a T-shirt in the pool. She might be inconsolable if she couldn't.

I stayed at camp that summer and fell in line soon after that meeting with Marge. I joined the swim team. I made friends with most of the girls in my division, including Amy, one of my best friends to this day. It's as if Marge Cohn had dared me, said, "Go ahead, try to have a normal life," and I took that dare. I never once asked to wear a goddamned T-shirt in the pool.

"The big one hasn't stopped eating since we sat down."
—An old lady at a friend's bat mitzvah

In her defense (I guess?), she didn't say it *to* me, only *near* me, but she was loud, and I was often on the lookout for offenders, spoiling for a fight. It was true—I hadn't stopped eating since we sat down. The kids' dais had bowls of Hershey's Kisses everywhere, exactly the kind of contraband I gobbled up as much as I could when I was out from under my parents. Even at thirteen, I was pretty spunky, so I shot the woman—my elder, somebody's grandmother—a look that said I had heard her and would make her pay. Caught, she smiled and said, "I could just watch you kids dance all day!" I smiled back and knew she wouldn't talk about me again.

"That's a puffy sweater, huh?"
—A frat boy in the dining hall my
first week at Boston University

It was a rhetorical question, and it was accompanied by his hand on my back. I was having dinner with new friends in the Warren Towers dining hall, and it was fraternity rush, when hopeful pledges sat together for every meal and did whatever humiliating tasks were demanded of them. As you've already seen from this book and maybe know from your own experience, sometimes people stumble into an insult unwittingly; sometimes they wield a certain kind of inappropriate curiosity;

but occasionally, as terrible as it is to hear, people are jerks for no good reason. You can be sitting there, a kind and empathic person, when suddenly, someone you assume to also be kind and empathic (because you assume that of everyone) turns out not to be. There is no point to their cruelty other than the cruelty itself. They are vampire kin.

This guy was wearing a bandanna like he was in a biker gang, as were all his tablemates, though he was more likely a cosplaying tough from a wealthy suburb of New York or New Jersey. He had that look about him, like the guys I grew up with: those sociopathic dead-eyed pricks who traveled in packs.

It was a quick moment, the frat boy's touching me and smiling while he did it—"That's a puffy sweater, huh?"—and he was gone before I fully realized what had happened. One of the girls at my table asked with a titter, "*What* did he say?" I told her I didn't know, laughing too. I needed the moment to be over and playing along seemed like the quickest way. Sitting there with my new friends, doing my closest approximation of a normal college student having a normal college meal, his intrusion shook me.

You might be wondering, with so many years of practice, how do you not get used to your body? But there are moments when I am struck as if for the first time: *This back, this dense lump clinging to me like a barnacle, it's always been with me and always will be; how do I get rid of it, I can't, I can't, I can't.* In those moments, instead of fighting or fleeing, I freeze.

"Wow, the right one is so much bigger!"
—A stranger in a shoe store

This may be my earliest memory of someone I didn't know talking about my body in front of me as if I weren't attached to it. I was little, shopping for shoes with my mom, and I'm sure neither of us was having fun. Shoe shopping was a particular kind of misery in the 1980s. The styles of the day were not amenable to feet like mine, which are flat, wide, and slightly different sizes, both big. My mom's response to the curious onlooker who had remarked on the difference in my feet was ferocious—"You think I don't know that?"—which in retrospect sounds more like a vexed plea for a break than a defense of me. Today I have no doubt that my mother's response would be, "Yeah, well, your face could stop a clock," which is one of her favorite insults for people she can't stand.

"Who's this? Oh! You look different from behind!"
—My boyfriend Henry's mom

When sweater coats came along as a trend in the late '90s, it was as if they'd been sent from the heavens just for me. If I couldn't walk around in a full suit of armor or giant opaque bubble, a piece of clothing that was practically a blanket was the next best thing. I bought as many as I could and did not take them off until the mid-aughts, when they were pilled, faded, and long out of style. I was wearing one the first time I met Henry's mom, at her sister's house for Christmas. When she walked into the house, I was seated on the couch and I guess she saw what I wanted her to: my thin face, my long neck, the illusion that the sweater coat, not DNA, was responsible for my bulk. When she found me standing in the kitchen a little while later, the sweater coat's power faltered because I was at a new angle with no sentry. I felt her hands on my hips first, then saw her head peering around me as if I were a tree and she a child playing hide-and-go-seek. "Who's this?" she asked, then a beat: "Oh! You look different from behind!" At her new vantage point, she hadn't known who I was. The words tumbled out of her mouth uncensored as she tried to figure how the girl with the thin face from the couch could also be the person standing in front of her now.

I decided that I did not like my boyfriend's mother.

### "It's really my week!" —A massage therapist

It took me a very long time to buck up the courage to get a massage, and once I did, I decided to give a speech every time: explaining the specifics of my back and my legs, saying that I was mentioning it only so the massage therapist was not caught off guard, assuring the person that they would not hurt me. (I recently realized that massage therapists often *do* hurt me, because parts of my back are sensitive, so I'm working on figuring out why I'm so hell-bent on making sure they're more at ease than I am.) The usual response to my speech is something to the effect of "Thank you for letting me know," or the terser "Okay, got it."

This particular woman was uncomfortable as soon as I started delivering my speech, I could just tell. There was an energy in the room that was not welcoming or good. I should have left, but those of us who were ever forced to diet or tend toward people-pleasing are good at denying and defying our instincts. By the time leaving occurred to me as an option, I was already under the sheets, naked.

When she said what she did—"It's really my week!"— I asked what she meant. "Well," she told me, "yesterday I had a woman who said, 'Don't touch over here, I have a clot; and don't touch here, I have a plate.'" I wanted to say it sounded like it was really *that* woman's week, but now here I was, another imperfect specimen dumped on the table. Poor thing, I probably should have offered to get up and give *her* a massage.

She kept talking while poking at me gingerly. Nobody wants the massage therapist to talk unless it's to say, "How's the pressure?" or "Everything all right?" or "This is the most fun I've ever had giving a massage, thank you so much!" But I especially did not want this person to tell me a story about someone she knew whose legs ended up different sizes like mine after she "had her menses." I remember that part distinctly because I honestly still don't know what the fuck she was talking about, and I also never, ever want anyone to say the word "menses" to me again.

Our hour together ended prematurely—she was so clearly flustered by my body that twenty minutes of perfunctory kneading was apparently all she could manage—and she left without saying a word. When I got to the checkout desk, I found that she hadn't charged me. I called later to complain anyway.

"What's on your back?" —An actor at a cover shoot

This was always my least-favorite collection of strung-together words, even before the vampire, because of its implication that there is some actual back beneath all the not-my-back. It suggests that if I only excavated deep enough, I'd be able to find my real back, the one that looks like everybody else's. Only, this *is* my real back, in the same way a shell does not house a turtle but is the turtle itself.

It happened on the set of my very first photo shoot, for a magazine you've never heard of that was privately funded by a husband and wife who had no publishing experience. Though I was making a four-hundred-dollar-a-month stipend and my bosses got copies of all our incoming and outgoing emails and we kept getting kicked out of offices for failure to pay rent, the job was fun in the way that first jobs are when you're in your twenties and hustling. Between takes, we were all sitting around chatting, and the actor just asked: "What's on your back?" My coworkers were there, as were the photographer, a stylist, the hair-and-makeup team. I had an audience, and the person speaking was our guest of honor; there was no way to ignore it.

"It's a condition I was born with," I responded, and she said, "Oh, you looked so warm, I was jealous."

It was a quick save, the only thing she could think of, I guess. Maybe it's possible she really thought I had a blanket wrapped around my midsection under my jacket? She was lovely when I interviewed her for our cover story later in the week, so I forgave her for basically telling me that I looked nice and toasty because of all the cozy layers of weird fat enveloping my body.

"That's not you, is it?" —A photography professor

In my last semester of college, I took Photography 101 as an elective and loved it. I had long been obsessed with magazines, mainly for the pictures. Every month I'd give my haul a cursory read, back to front, then take each book apart for its photos, adding to the collage assembled on the wall of my room: a zoomed-in glittery blue eye peeking out over here, the painfully thin appendages of models splayed like ragdolls there. The world inside magazines was perfect, and I wanted to literally inhabit it.

We were packing up to leave the photo lab when the professor fixed her stare on the bulgy parts of my torso, which she had apparently not noticed before. I didn't respond because I hadn't understood the question. I was dressing like a raver then: gigantic jeans, T-shirts over long-sleeve T-shirts. My goal, without realizing it, was to hide, but the professor had found me. That day, for some reason, even though it was the middle of the semester, she noticed that my body did not look like the body she'd assumed I had, and she had questions.

When I didn't produce an answer, she tried to find her own, by reaching out and running her fingers down my side, slowly and softly, as if I were covered in Braille. I stood there, frozen, while my teacher touched me in front of other students. As my eyes brimmed with tears, she realized what she'd done and snatched back her hand. By the time she caught me in the hallway to apologize, I was crying and angry. "Don't worry about it," I barked. "It's been happening my entire life." I remember feeling very dramatic as I stormed off, which I liked.

---

"I'd drill a hole in her hump and fuck the hole."
—An AOL commenter

---

Spoiler: This is not a meet-cute.

In 2009, I took my first stab at writing publicly about my body in a personal essay in *Marie Claire* titled "What the Guys I Date Don't Know." The article was about the ways in which dating is hard for me, and some of those ways are the same as for everybody else: Sometimes my dates bored me. Sometimes they were bad kissers. My problems with dating aren't *all* about my body, as I am but a human who inhabits a body, and my reactions to men aren't always kind or generous, for the same reason. The essay let all of that show.

I felt ready and elated to have such a major publication printing my work, but what I had not anticipated was that AOL would pick up the story and place it on its home page. The story went viral, which is of course what every writer wants, but I was not prepared. Agents fought to represent me; the person I signed with ultimately told me that she would have an easier time selling my book if I could find a boyfriend. (We both failed at our respective assignments.) Many readers of the essay reached out to say they thought I was "brave" and "inspiring." Others found me irritating, egotistical, ugly, not worthy of oxygen. Some readers—who I am quite confident are now thriving men's-rights activists—found it galling that I had complaints about my dating experiences at all: I should clearly be grateful that anyone would go out with me ever.

I wrote the essay to be understood and get published. I naively never imagined the many ways it could be weaponized against me.

The article got hundreds of comments that I promised myself I wouldn't read but of course did, and this is the one that made me contact AOL to say I felt personally threatened. Hole-in-the-back fucking felt just a little too specific. The site moderator closed down commenting on the post and removed everything that was there, including this graphic love note.

> "It must be really hard for you. I have a
> fifteen-year-old and she's very self-conscious."
> —Another. Fucking. Doctor.

You'd expect them to know better, right? All the things they've seen, conditions they've treated. But here's a secret nobody tells you: Doctors are just *people,* and many people are terrible. A friend had recommended this GP when I needed a physical to start grad school. Now look, it's possible that for someone who hadn't yet accepted her body, any mention of it (and, specifically, its difference and implicit inferiority) might have hit harder than intended, but for the love of god, are you not *al-*

*ready* your most vulnerable when you're sitting in a paper gown being examined by a stranger? This doctor's prodding me to acquiesce that I *must* be self-conscious felt like an attack. Also, I was not fifteen, like her dumb daughter, and I hated her insinuation that we were the same.

I couldn't tolerate it. The ribbons of sobs emerged uncontrollably. I shouted at the doctor to get away from me, not to touch me. She left the room and I got dressed. On the way out of the office, the receptionist saw me crying and asked, "Honey, what happened?" and I shouted, "Your boss is a bitch!"

I ended up, at twenty-two, back at my pediatrician's to get my grad school medical clearance.

---

"I know that your condition is going to be a barrier for me."
—A guy I'd been on one date with

---

He was that straightforward, and I have the proof, because this man emailed me after finding the now ubiquitous *Marie Claire* article. "I know that your condition is going to be a barrier for me," he wrote. "My condition is that I'm excessively, stupidly, self-damagingly fastidious with dating (I once ended a relationship because I couldn't stand the way the other person laughed), and I often find it impossibly hard to get past things that I'm not attracted to."

See what he did there? He repeated the word "condition" for narrative flair. We both have conditions. *My* condition is that I am deformed; *his* condition is that he is a dick (paraphrasing).

Anyway, he went on: "I want to accuse myself of shallowness, but at the same time, I think it's right to acknowledge an honest reaction to physical facts. . . . I guess this is the long way of saying that I don't think we can pursue a romantic relationship, in spite of all the things I like about you."

Again, we'd been out *once*.

This was what I'd dreaded my entire life: Someone I was attracted to and liked, who I had already made out with, was rejecting me because of my body, and not only that, he was *telling* me. Although he wasn't proud of it, he said, my body made our dating impossible. He could not get past it, he said.

Whether because of K-T or ADHD, I am often colorblind to red flags, and I realized in retrospect that he'd waved loads of them I either missed or willfully ignored. As we sat side by side at a Williamsburg bar on our date, he had looked at me, smiled, rolled his shoulders back in a way that meant I was supposed to follow, and said, "Posture." He also wouldn't stop fishing for my last name, a telltale when someone who's met you on a first-names-only dating site wants to do Google recon.

I'd been on more dates than I could count at this point, with varying degrees of success. I'd slept with a handful of men and made out with probably close to a hundred of them. Good dates, bad dates, medium dates, dates I don't even remember going on—I'd had them all. But I'd never had this.

Men had said things before, of course. A person couldn't go out with as many people as I did and *not* have somebody say something. Two different men, for example, mentioned my hands. One said, "I feel like you have spaces between your fingers that I don't have." The other said, "Your fingers are so weird!" I made out with both of them. I did not make out with the first person in my life to point out the finger spaces, my childhood orthopedic surgeon, Dr. Myers. He'd mentioned them nonchalantly during an otherwise standard visit, and at ten I looked down at my hands as if for the first time and realized he was right: My fingers are more spaced out than other people's, so when I crunch them together, there are little teardrop gaps I cannot make disappear.

In his email, this man I'd been on one date with said that although he was impressed with my bravery in writing about my deformity, it made him feel "a suffocating weight." He ended his letter with two questions: Could we be friends? And was I rolling my eyes at him?

I cried and cried when I got the email. I cried for a lost opportunity, for what I worried would be a life of forever lost opportunities. I cried because as much as I hated this guy, I worried that he was right: I wasn't good enough. I didn't deserve to be loved.

Then I got angry. When he'd corrected my posture, I wish I'd said, "You try sitting up straight with uneven butt cheeks and two curves in your spine, motherfucker." Pointless, and yet I regretted not putting in his place someone who was so eager to put me in mine.

I never responded to his email, but I did see him at a local café not long after. He positioned himself behind a column so that he was partially concealed, and I liked knowing he was uncomfortable. I liked knowing that he was the one who felt the need to hide from me. I liked knowing, eventually—and really, truly believing—that he was a bullet I dodged, not the other way around.

"Next time, could she wear something more flattering?"
—A *Today* show producer

I got the message secondhand, from the publicist at *Entertainment Weekly*, where I was working in 2017. I'd just done my first *Today* show spot, a pop culture quiz with Kathie Lee Gifford. I was good at TV, the kind of person they call "a natural." I had loads of experience from my previous gig as editor in chief of *Time Out New York*. My first-ever TV segment had been four minutes live standing under the Brooklyn Bridge recounting every detail of four hand-curated Independence Day deals for a reporter who couldn't hide how impressed he was with my charm and capability for recall. When people asked afterward if I'd been nervous, I said yes because that's what you're supposed to say, but I wasn't really nervous at all.

Over the course of my tenure at *Time Out*, I became the go-to editor in town to weigh in on local events (Washington Square Park Pillow Fight) and trends (artists fleeing Williamsburg for Bushwick) and round-ups (Best Donuts in the Five Boroughs). Producers at local outlets started asking me to do weekly and monthly segments about things to do in the city, and I'd gotten to thinking that maybe TV could be my next career. I loved everything about it: creating the lineups; the rapport I struck with the anchors; the attention it got me on social media and occasionally in person, when people would stop to ask if I was that girl from that thing. My omnipresence on local TV had led a couple of production companies to reach out about collaborating and even scored me a meeting with execs at Bravo who told me they liked to have people on standby in case Andy Cohen ever needed a fill-in.

For my first appearance on *Today,* I'd chosen a beaded Matthew Williamson babydoll and a cool pair of Loeffler Randall sandals over tights. I was happy with how I looked, and when I nailed the segment, I was elated. But apparently, I hadn't fooled this producer. I was in the big leagues now, and they had better eyesight.

I had to leave my desk when I got the email asking me to wear something more flattering, because our offices were glass and I was crying. *This stupid fucking body.* My always adversary, ready and waiting to ruin everything, my perpetual dream crusher. I was so angry at it.

For my second *Today* segment, with Willie Geist, I wore a jumpsuit with a black leather jacket over it. I was too self-conscious and flummoxed to pick anything else, so I added layers, going in the opposite direction of where the producer had asked me to, into something *less* flattering, whatever that means. I wasn't invited back and never asked why.


I could make ten, twenty, thirty more lists with completely different entries of the things people have said about my body. I could also make an infinite number of lists comprised of the looks I clock on the street, especially when I'm wearing a miniskirt or a tank top. I have no idea how many lists I could make about the once-removed implications, like the way the well-meaning greeters at the hospital where I get my monthly iron infusions always helpfully ask if I need directions to the four-teenth floor, which is the maternity ward. I have no idea how many lists I could make of the conversations that happen once I leave a room.

There was a time when the commentary felt—was—unceasing, not a list so much as a stream, ebbing and flowing but always, always coming. I was inundated. Which meant that I was always, always on alert. Or maybe it's the other way around. Chicken or egg. Maybe my vigilance was a beacon.

But there's another list, too: of compliments I've gotten about my face and even about my body. Those legs? A first date once told me I had great ones. He already knew they were dif-ferent sizes—he, too, had found the *Marie Claire* article and applauded my bravery; it made him like me *more,* he said. A different man once walked up to me in a bar to compliment my nose. Lots of gals I don't know have told me I have beautiful arms, for we women do this sort of thing, unbidden, for one another.

I have been told I have magnetism. People have stopped me on the street or leaned over to say some version of "Hey, I just wanted to tell you, I love your vibe." I am cocky enough to believe them: They love my vibe. I love my vibe, too! Hearing it gives me a little hit of dopamine.

*Good god, she's obsessed with herself,* may be what you're thinking right now, but I hope not. The point I am trying to make is that, for me, the real challenge has been in not depend-ing so much on the nice things to counteract the ugly ones, and not hanging so very much of my self-worth on what other peo-ple think of me, a gargantuan task for any person. Wanting to feel whole was the ultimate goal. First, it was important to admit to myself that as much as I hated the attention my body brought, I loved the attention my face got. Today, it gets much less—the skin sags, my formerly sharp jaw is now soft, I've lost that ethereal glow of youth men feast upon as if it were catching—but I see now it was a crutch as much as my body was a perceived obstacle. My body was a barrier for me, too. The hardest part has been the work I've had to do to fortify myself so that my foundation doesn't shake when people say anything—good or bad—because why should it? It's *my* fucking foundation.

# Handy-Dandy Flowchart

## So You've Noticed Someone with an Unconventional Body, Now What?

Even those of us born with weird bodies and/or a surfeit of compassion aren't immune to the occasional misstep, and you may be thinking right now, *Fuck, I'm a body commenter—I'm a goddamned body commenter!* Fear not, I'm here to help.

Take a moment to think about whether you routinely remark on other people's bodies without consent or invitation. If the answer is yes, snip out this helpful guide and keep it in your pocket. Become *more* aware of people's bodies, but in a different way. Take note of the size and shape of booths and the sturdiness of chairs in relation to the folks you're with. Find out whether there are stairs wherever you're going and think about how that will impact your companions. If you're traveling with friends, especially those in bigger bodies who have been shamed their whole lives for taking up too much room, consider that when you make your plans. (Like, perhaps don't schedule a helicopter ride that requires passengers to weigh themselves unless you've heard your friend say, "There is nothing I enjoy more than getting weighed in front of people.") If you can't be aware and empathic in an organic way yet, fine, baby steps, but at least don't be a jerk.

It's also important to note that on one hand, here's me, telling you to keep your dirty mouth shut when curiosity bubbles up inside and starts catapulting words of inquiry; on the other, there are disability advocates who talk about the joy of polite, curious (but not gawking, judgmental) asking. On the other hand (I have three hands!), everybody is different. What I'm saying is: Be aware. My chart can help you regardless, especially any reformed assholes or people still working on it. I will give you grace, reformees, just work harder and faster.

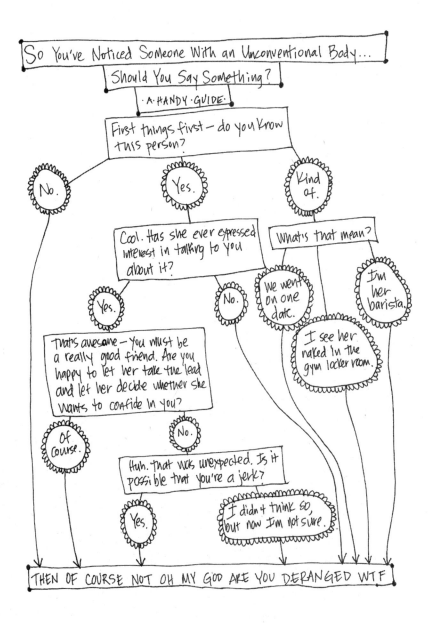

# 3.

## Nose Job Gym Is Apparently Not Something Everyone Grew Up With?

was eight or nine, and my parents explained the procedure to me as well as they could.

"They're just going to suck everything out," my mom said.

"Like a vacuum?" I asked.

"Exactly," my dad confirmed. "In fact," he said with a laugh, "I'll go get the Hoover and we can do it right now." He pinched me on the cheek, our stand-in for a hug for as long as I can remember, and that was the end of the conversation.

In 1985, the words "suction lipectomy," or "liposuction," as we would come to know it, meant nothing to me but seemed to mean not much more to the grown-ups. It was not yet something real housewives did between Pilates and Botox. The procedure was so new that when we'd first scheduled the surgery, I was meant to have a different one—I have no idea what it was; I remember only that I would be under anesthesia for something like seven hours, which was more dangerous—and in that small window between marking the calendar and operation day, liposuction had emerged as an option. I guess it's possible I'm one of the first people to have ever had it.

My plastic surgeon, Dr. Leitch, told us you could only do a little liposuction at a time, so I would need several. The plan was for him to make tiny incisions in my back and suck out the fat through each one. At my next surgery, he'd do some more. Then more. And more. I didn't know how much sucking could be done, if the sucking could go on forever, if my life could be one big suckfest.

I understood very little about the surgery, just that it was part of the job of making me smaller and less lumpy. My body had always been simultaneously a locus of concern for my family and something we didn't really discuss. This was no different. I had been seeing doctors for as long as I could remember, since before I ever thought to ask why, and even though I knew that not every kid had as many medical appointments as I did, it all seemed weirdly normal.

I also always knew I wouldn't simply be going for observational visits in perpetuity. There was a goal, and it was likely going to include an operating table. I was nervous about the needles and the fact that I would probably have to be weighed at some point, but not much else worried me.[*] I specifically re-

---

[*] As an adult, I have no fear of needles. I watch my veins with curiosity as nurses draw blood, never flinching as they plunge vaccines into my biceps. I stoically self-injected during the process of freezing my eggs. Funny, how the thing that scares you can become what you're drawn to or at least indif-

member thinking that if I concentrated extremely hard on ignoring the prospect of surgery, I could forestall it forever, but otherwise I was yielding and pliant.

I dreaded the physical pain of surgery but didn't consciously feel any emotional or psychological turmoil. I wasn't worried that having to go into the hospital for liposuction was an indication that I was inadequate. I was not angry that other people got to make such a big decision on my behalf. It didn't occur to me to feel upset that my body was going to be intruded on so catastrophically. I trusted grown-ups implicitly, and more than that, I was a pretty self-assured little kid; surgery was a bummer, but it didn't feel like it was ruining my life. In a lot of ways, it was unremarkable.

Certainly nobody ever said, "You are different and we need to fix you." Neither did anyone say, "This kind of stinks, and to be honest we're not sure if it's the right decision, and PS adults may seem like they know what they're doing, but we're as clueless as everyone else." That time of my life, at least in my memory, is marked mostly by its lack of words. I don't know that this was a mistake and also don't know that it wasn't. Big deal, I had to have surgery. I acquiesced and didn't ask questions and no one gave answers and we all sort of just got on with things.

Sure, in the weeks before the operation, my mom was more anxious than usual (this was impressive), and because it was the era of hemophiliac Ryan White, who got AIDS from a transfusion, my dad donated blood ahead of time in case I

---

ferent about. I never came to love scales, but I did, like most women, become obsessed with them.

needed it. Since I didn't *really* mind my appearance, I wasn't even particularly excited about the prospect of transformation, though I did have a secret wish I'd come out looking like Alyssa Milano.

Mostly, I just wanted it over. "It," thanks to liposuction, was now "them." I wanted *them* over, all the operations I had to have.

The day of my first surgery, it was drizzling when we departed Long Island for the Bronx, where all my doctors were, and as we turned off our street, a woman in another car skidded and nearly plowed into us. My dad got out to make sure she was okay. It didn't occur to me to wonder if I was okay. It definitely didn't occur to me to run. I wasn't that kind of kid.

At the hospital, as I waited to be admitted, a grown-up sitting next to me asked what I was in for, casually, as if she'd inquired whether it was still raining. I explained that I was there to have an operation on my back because I had a cosmetic disorder. My mother didn't interrupt but was livid afterward: "How could she ask you that? What if you had *cancer*?"

Is "cosmetic disorder" a thing? It's what I've always called Klippel-Trenaunay, and I can't figure out if I made it up or maybe my parents or doctors did. It seems impossible that it's an actual medical term, for what is "cosmetic disorder" if not a euphemistic way to say "got beat with the ugly stick"? Even if it is real, I'm not sure whether it's a good or bad thing that I equated major vascular abnormalities, which did actually affect my health in some ways, with an aesthetic defect.

As I lay on a gurney just outside the OR, a nurse asked about my macramé anklet—even as young and doped up as I was, I was aware that she was just being kind, trying to distract me with small talk—and I promised to make her one and bring it next time, when I came back for my second surgery. I did not follow through with this promise.

Afterward, when I came to in the recovery room, I was mortified that my hospital gown was missing and confused because my thigh was throbbing. "Dr. Leitch was able to take a little out of your thigh and tush!" my mom happily informed me. I felt neutral about the news then but wonder now whether someone should have checked with me first: "Hey, while we're working on your back, is it okay to play around with some other parts?" Nobody had asked for my permission for any of it, so I guess why start now?

I stayed in the hospital for a night or two, receiving a string of visitors and cards from school that my parents must have brought with them. My aunt Margie and uncle Alan arrived with a fruit basket, and my aunt said, "We were going to bring loads of junk food, but we figured that would defeat the point!"

My roommate was loud and chatty and I felt bad that I found her annoying, because she had a tumor; I only had a cosmetic disorder.

Doctors I'd never seen before and would never see again came in and out of my room to undo my compression wrap and give lessons at my back. I was the chalkboard. Dr. So-and-So and Dr. Such-and-Such would gingerly turn me on my side, unstick the Velcro, and, with med students in tow, appraise me like a piece of art. I was a rare specimen and a special treat. I would have minded except that I was grateful to be momen-tarily un-mummified.

Everyone has things from childhood they take for granted as normal, that they don't realize are out of the ordinary until they tell someone else and see a blank stare or pure shock reflected back at them. For example, the children of a New York crime boss went to my high school, and my friend Maura's brother hitched a ride with them every day. Each morning, the dad would start the car before letting the kids get in to make sure it didn't blow up. Once he did, off to school they'd go.

Is liposuction my exploding car? Sometimes I'll be talking about it and realize how strange it sounds. Oh. Not everyone did that. Not every eight-year-old had plastic surgery. My ther-apist, Marilyn, would tell you that of course I know it was out of the ordinary and of course I'm angry about it, and why—*why?!?*—can't I acknowledge that I endured a trauma, to which I say, WHAT DOES SHE KNOW? (A lot. She knows a lot.)

But I do have trouble with the word "trauma." I struggle to wrap my brain around its pertaining to me when I have friends who have endured what I consider to be real and worse tragedies (poverty, rape, marital suicide, cancer). Though in the logical recesses of my brain I know there is more than enough to go around, that pain is not pie, it's hard to reconcile that anything traumatic ever happened to me when I grew up with so much. "You have to say thank god" has always been my mom's refrain anytime we see someone without a home or otherwise down and out. I knew early on that I had to count my blessings.

I've been told I sound disconnected when I describe my surgeries. I *feel* disconnected. It's like it happened to someone else, and my memories are fractured and specific. To this day, I dissociate at doctors' appointments. The body is so good at protecting itself from repeated attack that I often don't realize the gravity of medical news until much later. A doctor will tell me that my heartbeat is irregular or that my lung is filled with fluid or that an untreated UTI has resulted in pyelonephritis and my kidney is, as we speak, turning to pus, and I will say, "Uh-huh, okay." I won't panic, even when the thing I'm supposed to do next is get to an emergency room immediately. The ability to not panic in a crisis does come in handy, especially when people are prone to telling you alarming things about your body.

I will of course panic later, when the feelings back up and I realize that I should have panicked earlier and *what the hell is wrong with me that I didn't panic?!?*

Indifference to doctors as an adult isn't the worst thing, considering the contempt I had for them as a kid; that I go to the doctor at all is a miracle. I hated Dr. Myers, the orthopedic surgeon of weird-finger fame, who once let a group of med students into the room to examine my naked body without asking permission *and* made me wear a back brace in high school. I hated the male gynecologist my parents took me to when I was twelve and having excessively heavy periods, because the idea of a man poking around down there made me want to crawl out of my skin. I hated my very sweet pediatricians because they always, always wanted to talk about my weight.

Once, as an adult, I asked my mother about all the doctors and surgeries, if it really was as straightforward as I remembered, that it was just about improving my looks. "It was just about your appearance," she confirmed, and I could tell she thought she was reassuring me: There was no secret health hazard at the root of it; I wasn't in danger; there was no absolute need for the surgery; I was okay.

But her answer only disoriented me more, and I didn't ask anything else, like why she and my dad and my doctors felt the need to change my appearance. Were they afraid I'd get picked on? Did they think they were making my life easier? Did my body repel them? Was it a foregone conclusion in the 1970s that if your kid popped out deformed, you would do everything in your power to fix her even if it wasn't strictly necessary? Even if all she had was a cosmetic disorder?

The day I was released from the hospital, I inhaled the smell of my dad's Polo sweater as he helped me into the car. It was raining again, and the wool reeked like an animal. I received an Apple IIc as a surgery gift, and when I broke my previous record in *Where in the World Is Carmen Sandiego?,* my dad, not thinking, gave me a congratulatory slap on my still sore and stitched-up back, and I yelped.

When I returned to school, Kevin Cryer, a classmate who was mean to me when we were younger but by then had become a good friend, approached me sheepishly: "Warren Levy said you had surgery on your butt. That's not true, is it?"

I had no idea how he knew. My ass is still deformed enough in my forties that I can tell you with certainty Warren Levy didn't suspect surgery on my butt because I suddenly had a normal-looking one, but I was mortified. In my small town, everybody knew about my cosmetic disorder—my "back problem," as I sometimes called it, like I'd slipped a disc—but surgery on my *butt*? That was a humiliation I could not bear, and Kevin didn't want to either.

"That's so crazy," I lied with a laugh. "I just had surgery on my back!"

"Okay, that's what I thought," he said, and we were both relieved.

I'm sure denial was a survival technique, but where I grew up, Long Island's Five Towns, definitely aided in my ability to disconnect from how kind of nuts it is that I had plastic surgery as a child. Being from the Five Towns brought certain associations; the most obvious is apparent from its name: Saying you lived in the "Five Towns" (big *F*, big *T*) was meant to give the impression that they were the only five towns that existed, or at least the only ones that mattered.

Our insular Jewish community sat on a small slice of Long Island's South Shore, just outside New York City. We were pleasantly shielded from antisemitism, though my rabbi had the numbers on his arm, and somebody once spray-painted a swastika and the word "Jewlett" on the side of Hewlett High School, where my mom taught and I eventually went.

During most of my adolescence, Hewlett Harbor, Hewlett Bay Park, and Hewlett Neck sat in the top five richest neighborhoods in *U.S. News & World Report*'s annual ranking. Most of the kids who lived within those exclusive hamlets would make sure you knew it, for example by never just saying they lived in "Hewlett." They'd tack on the Harbor, Bay Park, or Neck to make sure you understood that they did not reside in one of the regular-size houses in the main part of town but were instead cloistered inside a gargantuan waterside monstrosity, with their own boat tethered to their own dock or a Rolls in the driveway. My friend Daniella had an indoor pool and a front lawn so big, sometimes she'd come outside to find people picnicking because they'd mistaken it for a public garden.

We lived in North Woodmere, a much less fancy neighborhood with cookie-cutter houses a ten-minute walk from the Queens border, where the planes about to land at Kennedy swooped what felt like a little too low. North Woodmere is a fabricated section of a much bigger village called Valley Stream. So desperate were the settlers of North Woodmere to be part of the exclusive Five Towns, they renamed it. Woodmere is one of the Five Towns. *North* Woodmere is one of the Five Towns Asterisk. We got in on a technicality, which is a good way to describe the way I've felt for a lot of my life (*We Got In on a Technicality: The Carla Sosenko Story*).

In addition to Hewlett and Woodmere, the other three towns comprising the five are Cedarhurst, Lawrence, and Inwood; Inwood was an anomaly in that it wasn't mostly Jewish or white or wealthy, and most of us in the four towns didn't know anyone in the fifth. In the 1980s, the four towns of the Five adopted the country's more-is-more attitude as if it were patriotic duty, and we never learned about the Indigenous tribes that had populated the island before us.

The Five Towns *loved* plastic surgery. By the time I got to high school in 1990, we had a special gym class to accommodate those students who were healing from recent rhinoplasty. For many, the surgery was a belated bat mitzvah gift, and nobody seemed to appreciate the irony of celebrating the sacred rite by turning everyone's Jewish bumps into exaggerated gentile slopes. Nose Job Gym was, to quote *Clueless*, for the students whose doctors didn't want balls flying at their noses. Instead they'd spend forty-two minutes in our school's weight room lazily pumping the pedals of stationary bikes and engaging in other contact-free forms of exercise. Sometimes a chin job accompanied the nose job to make sure the dimensions of the face weren't thrown off and rendered accidentally Picassoesque. These surgeries were always performed over summer vacation or winter break so nobody had to endure the humiliation of bandages and black eyes. You never knew who was going to come back to school with a brand-new face.

I didn't want a nose job. In fact, my deformity made me mostly immune to the more trifling obsessions of my peers: Hook noses. Cellulite. Big butts. I couldn't tell you what a supposedly "good butt" looked like because any one that had cheeks that matched looked pretty good to me. Cellulite? Who cares! I didn't even know what the striations that appeared one day on my own body were until it occurred to me to ask a friend, and she told me they were stretch marks. While everyone else was obsessing about the size of their nostrils and thighs, I was focused on the parts of the body most people ignore—the back, the calves—which means we were all doing the same thing, just differently. Were any of us happy?

I've always said I had four operations, but my mother once said no, she was pretty sure I had three, and I trust her memory on this more than my own. I do know that the last operation happened in eighth grade, when I was twelve or thirteen, and the reason it was my last was because I decided it would be. Stopping was simple economics for me: Surgery meant enduring multiple needles, missing weeks of sports, and wearing that goddamned compression garment, all for, from what I could tell, the very slight excavation of some previously buried bones near the top of my back. Yes, I got a big present every time I had an operation (just as I'd always gotten a trip to the toy store and Epstein's deli after every doctor's visit), but in terms of what it was all meant to accomplish, I just wasn't convinced. What was the point of having a *slightly* less deformed butt than the one you started with? Who cared if the top of your back was just a little less fatty than before when a back isn't supposed to be fatty at all? I asked multiple times if Dr. Leitch could do anything to make my legs more symmetrical, and my mom said over and over that he couldn't, it was too dangerous to touch the legs. She gently prodded me to keep seeing him anyway, but I was not interested unless he could promise something more dramatic. If I was going to keep doing it, it needed to feel worth it.

It didn't.

Maybe there was more—a deep psychological revulsion or resentment of being "improved"—but either way, I was not going to do it anymore. At twelve or thirteen, I was the one who got to decide, I'm not sure why. An integral part of my life was gone in an instant. No more doctors. No more surgery. No more regular medical appraisals of my body. No more trips to the Bronx. It was over.

After so many years of medical intrusion, I was left a Frankenstein's monster, only incomplete. To this day I don't know which parts of me are the result of genetics and which were created by surgery; which are the foundation that was always there and which are man-made nicks and embellishments. For someone who can become agitated by an outfit she doesn't love or a crooked picture frame or a piece of furniture that doesn't quite go, this bothers me less than you might think. It doesn't bother me at all, actually. I don't know why.

It has occurred to me that medicine has likely come far enough that perhaps if I wanted to, I could revisit plastic surgery; maybe even my leg would be fair game now. I could make the improvement of my body my life's work, an ongoing project, maybe even performance art. But the idea of it exhausts me. Anytime I feel a little flare of *maybe,* it flames out fast. There are so many better things I could do with my time and money. And so I am left a work in progress that will never progress, like a construction site that broke ground, then lost its funding.

# 4.

## You Can't Spell "Trauma" Without "Ma"

At forty-seven, I am closer with my folks than is probably normal. I talk to my mom every day. Sometimes she calls me more than that. If we have dinner, I am instructed to text her when I get home, and I comply. When the subways get 1980s-level scary again, my parents command me to take Ubers everywhere and charge my rides to them. Yes, they are the stereotypical embodiment of hovering Jewish parents, but their care is genuine, and I appreciate it. Maybe they are the stereotype of parents who had a sick (but not really sick) kid. I don't know. They're the only parents I've ever had.

My friend Melissa, lamenting her own dad's disinterest in her life, recently said, with no ill will, "Try to imagine what it's like not to have parents who are obsessed with you." And though I'd never thought of it that way, I understood what she meant. She'd been there alongside my mother and father when they stayed up all night with me in the ER after I choked on a wishbone and needed an emergency endoscopy. She'd heard about the time I was having a panic attack and my mom immediately drove us out to Long Beach so I could take big gulps of salt air, then bought me an Isabel Marant coat to cheer me up. My parents are generous. They are givers. They are so caring. They would drop literally anything they were doing to help me if I needed it or even just wanted it, and would do—and have done—the same for many of my friends. They are who I would choose all over again.

Memory is such a slippery thing—it can be hard to remember what things were once like in contrast to what they're like now—but I don't think my parents today are the parents I grew up with, and I am not their daughter. They changed, I changed, multiple times. It was gradual, over the course of many years, so I can't explain how it happened exactly. I think I adjusted my boundaries, and they followed my lead.

My dad worked in Washington, D.C., when I was growing up, which took him away half of every week, so he felt mostly like a shadow, looming simultaneously giant and invisible to me. When he was home, it's the mercurialness I remember in my bones—the quiet tone shift that could level me, a sudden cold snap because I posed a statement as a question or a question as a statement or talked too fast or ate too much or spoke to him in a way he didn't like or didn't know the name of the lawyer who was impeaching Bill Clinton (Henry Hyde, I'll never forget now).

But I also remember him as the more playful parent. My father was the one who cleaned my newly pierced ears when I was seven because my mother found ear piercing "barbaric" and couldn't stomach it; he was the one who dutifully took my picture when I wanted to enter a *Sassy* magazine modeling contest; he was the one who would suggest I invite friends over for a barbecue, grilling for the five or ten teenagers who had materialized out of nowhere. Our relationship wasn't perfect, but it was relatively simple: I was intimidated by my dad, in awe of my dad, and constantly seeking my dad's approval. When I picture myself in relation to him, I am perched atop a layer of eggshells, trying to find my footing, simultaneously desperate to disappear and to shine.

My relationship with my mom was more complicated, as girls' relationships with their mothers tend to be. My mom was the one who was always there, who didn't get to flee each week, and she was not as much fun. I remember her as tired, overworked, frustrated, stressed, and why wouldn't she be: She was parenting me by herself half of every week, teaching multiple classes of jerky high school kids, and worrying about her own mentally ill mother.

The most consistent thing I remember about my mom from my childhood is her nervousness. Sometimes she had panic attacks in her sleep and woke up screaming. Other times, I'd hear her tell my dad, "I don't feel real," which is a scary thing for a kid to hear a parent say. I am her only child and my dad's third, after my sister and brother, Cara and Michael, who are twelve and fourteen years older than I am and always lived with their own mom. My mother occasionally let slip a regret and resentment that she hadn't had a second kid, and I got the sense that a combination of factors had stopped her: financial insecurity, dissuasion from her own mother (I also made up a reason: "Look how the first one turned out, maybe don't press your luck"). In every photo of my mom and me, from when I am five or twelve or twenty-three or thirty or forty-seven, we are standing side by side, her hand outstretched and gently grasping my arm. She is always making sure we are close, that she can locate me, that I am okay, that I won't get away or lost or too far from her.

When my dad was in D.C., Monday through Wednesday or Wednesday through Friday, I occupied his place in my parents' bed. Then my father would return and I'd be shuffled back to my own bedroom. I can't remember how old I was when this stopped, but I wasn't a baby.

The fact that my mother was a teacher at my high school meant I could come upon her at the turn of any corner—and because she had worked there for so much longer than I'd been a student, I was the interloper. Having my mother so close had its pitfalls and benefits, and sometimes they were the same. During the years I was supposed to be wearing a back brace, I would swipe a spare set of my mom's car keys every morning. I'd wear the brace to school, then walk over to the faculty lot and deposit it in her trunk. Sometimes I'd see her in the halls and be caught, my slouching posture the proof of what I'd done. She'd frown or shake her head, but I didn't care. I was not going to wear that fucking brace. It was hot and heavy and uncomfortable, and it ruined all my outfits.

I do not remember my early relationship with my mother as

easy or organic, but as one of pushing and pulling, of homecoming and rejection. She was overinvolved and controlling and overprotective—in pre-K, to avoid sunburn, I had to sit under a tree when all the kids played, and my babysitter, Barbara Garrigan, drove me to and from school long after other kids were commuting solo—but my mom could also be so intermittently remote and removed from my inner life that my emotional stability always felt topsy-turvy. When I was in ninth grade, she found flash cards on which I'd scribbled half-baked thoughts about suicide (I was upset that John Ostrick, a junior I was infatuated with, did not seem interested in me), and she asked about them. "They're for an English project," I lied on the spot, and she bought it or said she did. I knew, even then, how strange it was that she didn't push for details. I remember thinking how easy it would have been for her to find out whether I was telling the truth from my teacher, who was her coworker and friend. But she didn't. I did not want her to—I was mortified—but I thought it odd that she hadn't.

At times, I think I must have seemed like an alien. My mother was petite and thin, a former dancer and ice skater, so I couldn't have looked anything like she'd have expected. She told me often that she'd given me the face she always wanted. I knew she thought I was prettier than she was, but we were tied because she was thinner.

She would try to foist upon me Lydia O'Leary Covermark, a thick concealer conceived by an artist with a birthmark on her face. My mom routinely extoled the virtues of Lydia O'Leary, and I understood why. I could picture her as a young woman in the '60s applying Covermark to minor annoyances like blemishes and under-eye bags before jetting off to hear folk music in the Village or chain-smoke at parties. She urged me repeatedly to try the concealer to cover up the sprawling jam-colored mess on my torso, but I couldn't be bothered. The name said it all, as if one or two self-contained marks were as much as this O'Leary chick could help with. There wasn't enough Covermark in the world to conceal me; if there had been, I would have been left practically invisible, and I wasn't yet interested in that.

I felt pressure, from both of my parents, to be smarter and better than anyone seemed to believe I could be. A running gag in our family was that at restaurants, I would be given the bill to pay at the front, but the catch was that I had to tell my parents ahead of time how much change I should get. I would stand there trying to subtract numbers in my head, getting increasingly flustered until sometimes I'd cry. At the same time, teachers would suggest moving me into honors math and my mom would refuse, telling them, "She doesn't like math, she won't do well." In tenth grade I finally persuaded her to let me try, but by then everyone else in the class had been taking honors for so long that I was unequivocally behind. I transferred myself out after one day.

My mother wasn't wrong—I *didn't* like math, and I *don't* succeed at things that don't interest me—and the flip side was that she let me lean into subjects I did like. By senior year of high school, I was no longer taking science and was simultaneously in AP Spanish, Italian 3, and French 1. In a lot of ways, my mother knew her kid. Sometimes that meant I was preemptively barred from anything she thought I would fail at, which taught me that things weren't worth trying unless you could guarantee your success. The message seemed to contradict other ones I was picking up—like that there was honor in trying to make a body smaller than it wanted to be and valiance in sticking out uncomfortable situations—and it all confused me.

Years later, Marilyn told me that kids who endure medical trauma are likely to be academic underachievers. I was happy to get an explanation for why I seemed to have so much more potential than I was ever able to realize. It was there, the promise, we could all see it, but I could never quite fly except in a few specific areas.

When my father wasn't in D.C., he and my mom couldn't or wouldn't keep their hands off each other. I wished for the type of parents some of my friends had: the kind that seemed more like brother and sister than life partners, or who coexisted with a quiet indifference, barely registering the other's presence when they happened to coincide in a room. What I would have given for parents who were disinterested in each other. "When you only have one kid, they're like luggage—you take them everywhere," my mom used to say. Everywhere was mostly the backseat of whatever car we had at the time on long road trips listening to Erasure and Prince and the Go-Go's and mixtapes friends had made me, absenting my mind into a fantasy world that disappeared me somewhere far away. In hotels, my parents found my discomfort funny. "Carla, go to your room," one would say with a laugh as they rolled around on the other bed, the implicit joke being that I had no room to go to, that I was stuck there. I would bury my head in a pillow and turn the other way.

I once heard them talking about their plan to die together in a plane crash when they were old; the logistics made no sense—they both hated flying, and who would be the pilot?—but its implication was clear: They were a unit and when they decided it was time to go, I would be someone else's problem. Even if it was just a fairy-tale dream, it made my place in our configuration clear.

I was a late bloomer, and I don't think it's just because I felt like a stranger in my body. Or, I don't think I felt like a stranger in my body just because I was born with a weird one. Feeling like a third wheel to my parents meant there was an aspect of romantic relationships that absolutely repelled me. As a preteen and teen and twentysomething and even thirtysomething, I was particularly sensitive to the experience of being left out and aware of the power I could wield by leaving out others. I became a skilled emotional terrorist, adept at icing out girlfriends who had the audacity to find boyfriends or someone else to supplant me. It happened organically: A new person would enter their lives and suddenly I hated my friend and had the desire to make her feel invisible to me. I was very good at it.

I felt a flash of rage when witnessing couples who were happy in a particular way, the kind that are spotlighted in *New York Magazine* features and the lead of the *New York Times* Wedding section, a way that feels designed to exclude, to rub it in our faces, to brag about how happy they are and how little they ever consider us. Those smug, self-satisfied assholes who expect the world to pay attention to how great they are together. I had nothing but antipathy for those people.

Isosceles triangle was my most familiar, repeated, uncomfortable shape, and I always felt like the shorted side.

I was in my late twenties when I went into therapy. There's a thing that happens to anyone who's doing real work with a good therapist: You become a time traveler. You exist in both the present and the past, but the people around you don't know that, so your trips back in time and their clandestine nature disorient them. Every week you are going in and digging up all the hurt and pain and mistakes from long ago, and you carry those memories, live grenades, with you in the present. The people in your life don't know that, so they are accidentally activating you all the time. Your parents don't know that on Wednesday morning you talked to your shrink for forty-five minutes about old resentments you didn't even realize you had, so that when you talk to them on Thursday, they are confused about why you are distant and cold.

Once I began time traveling, my mother paid most dearly for my trips, for even today, I remain somewhat intimidated by my dad, so much softer and less volatile than when I was growing up, but the sense memory remains.

During my time-hopping, a simple declarative sentence from my mother could inflame my deepest resentments. Often my reaction, an outsize snap not at all commensurate with whatever she had just said, would be followed by a sense of guilt and shame, then an apology. It was an exhausting cycle.

At the time, I was living in the same building as their Manhattan pied-à-terre, which they'd purchased when I was a sophomore in high school. (We went from not having much money to having a lot of it in what felt to me like an instant but had of course taken years of nonstop work and planning and saving by my parents.) I was in a different apartment, in a different tower, but my address became further reason for me to consciously separate myself from them. I was such a baby, I told myself, that even living on my own in my twenties I hadn't been brave enough to move beyond their building. How must that look to everyone? How weak must I seem? I decided my parents and especially my mother must have made me that way. That hand, always grasping my arm. I overcorrected what I felt was a mistake by deciding that the only way the arrangement could work was if I talked to them much, much less. I did not tell them my plan. I'm sure we still talked more than most adult children and their folks, but when you are as intertwined as we were, even the subtlest shift, even for just a few months, is perceptible.

My mother finally asked: "Are you ever going to tell me what I did?"

I was at work, on the copy desk at *Life & Style,* when she called, and I resented her for asking because it meant I not only had to endure her mistakes but also take responsibility for helping her process their effect.

"You really want to know?" time-travel me snarled. "Fine."

I went down to the parking lot and paced while telling her what she said she wanted to know.

I resented her unflagging attention to my weight and the fact that she'd essentially given me disordered eating.

It was the doctors, she said. It's what they wanted.

I really resented that she and my father were always all over each other; it had fucked me up.

She didn't have parents who loved each other. She thought it was a good thing for a child to see affection.

I don't remember what else I said. I know that examples of bad parenting sprang to mind like on a shopping list, itemized mistakes I didn't realize I'd been tallying. I know I felt guilty that I was brave enough to tell only my mom, not my dad, that she should have to take on so much responsibility by herself. I don't remember what else my mother said, either, except that she apologized. I was still angry and stayed that way for a time, but I think that was the day things started to turn around.

I'm making it sound much easier than it was, but this was the very beginning. The exact same therapy that had sent me traveling to the past taught me that I did not have the power to change it, and the responsibility wasn't mine to try. I knew that my parents had done the best they could and in so many ways had done an excellent job. I stopped looking at them in pieces, like groceries; I started to see them as a whole, the same way I was trying to do with myself. I also knew from therapy that the goal was not getting the people around me to change—what an impossible proposition that would be—but processing my own past to understand my present. This helped.

Our relationship to one another, in retrospect, had always been one of ebbs and flows. When I went away to college, we became closer. When I invited them back into my life after edging them out during therapy, my mother especially, closer still. Absence made all of our hearts grow fonder, and it made them more delicate with me, and me with them. They are the parents I dreamed of having when I was young. How lucky I am. They made some mistakes, but who gets out of childhood unscathed?

And my mother was sorry, which was crucial. It was something I'd always suspected, because one of her most frequent questions of me, often asked out of the blue, is, "Did you have a happy childhood?" I always tell her yes, because I did.

I'm conscious of the way my mother, older now, can drive me bonkers. I am certain (and have told her) that she also has ADHD. Hanging invisible in the air over any conversation with my mom are the carcasses of sentences that will forever go unfinished and only those of us who know her well are able to decipher. You learn to follow along. It is adorable and hilarious to people who aren't her daughter. It even charms me if I'm in the right mood. But if I'm not, it sets me topsy-turvy again because I'm searching for punctuation in the ether, and even though I can keep up, it doesn't mean I want to. If my dad scolds her for her tangents or interruptions, I am crazy-made but simultaneously protective and enraged on her behalf. My anxiety level after too much time with my parents is often high.

I still seek their approval in a way I'm not sure all adults do. In my late thirties, we took my sister's five kids to my childhood spot, Hot Skates, and my ability to roller-skate really, really well came right back. I made fast loops around the rink and even remembered how to cross my feet at the corners. I found myself looking for my dad on the carpet without knowing why. He waved me down and my heart jumped. "Help Brynn!" he said. My niece was clinging to the wall, and he wanted me to teach her how to skate. I didn't realize until he said it that what I'd been hoping for was some version of "I can't believe you're still such a good skater!" Little Me had never left Hot Skates; she'd been waiting all that time for some encouragement.

I still ask for something like permission to do certain things, telling them my plans—"I'm going to Mexico by myself"; "I turned down that job"—then trying to read their reactions and act accordingly depending on my mood (insecure and compliant or purposefully defiant). Though I am excessively independent in many ways, I feel incapable of making what I think of as real, important adult decisions on my own, and sometimes even not-important decisions. I wouldn't know how to buy an apartment without their help. I wouldn't know how to buy a car. If I complain of feeling exhausted and my mother suggests I cancel my plans and take it easy—"You're always running yourself ragged," she'll say—I will snap at her for infantilizing me while simultaneously knowing that because she has given me, a middle-aged woman, an out, when I inevitably do cancel, it will be because my mommy said I could. I still sometimes try to impress them, to prove that I am smart, that I'm not the girl who couldn't hack it in honors math or didn't know who Henry Hyde was.

Sometimes I still don't know which are my own fears and beliefs and which are my mother's implanted long ago—never live on the ground floor of a building; never buy a piece of clothing with stripes if the stripes aren't perfectly matched at the seam; never drink alcohol before seven P.M.; never buy a German car.

Every time the phone rings I worry that they have bad news. I am perpetually afraid of losing them. I have felt like this my entire life.

Did my parents do this to me? Did I do it to myself? Was it an inevitability that we would function this way when I was born with a weird congenital disorder and became glued to them in a way not every kid is? My guess is yes and also no. It was inevitable given the way we functioned as a family unit, which was only inevitable because we made it so, like any family, which is made up of individuals with individual fears and drives and dynamics and histories.

Those years I spent sleeping in my mom's bed, I think that was her decision. I wouldn't have realized that were it not for a conversation with my sister, Cara. We were talking about the fact that I didn't go to sleepaway camp until I was twelve, when she and my brother had gone as little kids.

"I think the 'rents knew I would freak out when I got there," I said.

"No, I don't think that was it," Cara said. "I don't think your mother was ready to let you go."

That reoriented things for me. All this fear and not-being-able-to-ness that I'd always thought of as mine wasn't, maybe.

It's hard to overstate how much I love my parents, how in awe and proud of them I am. What they've done with their lives, professionally and creatively and financially, especially when they were not given the leg up I was, amazes me. That they are as good as they are—excessively good and fair and thoughtful, when so many people are bad or just average. I know how lucky I am. I have the parents other people want—friends beg for dinner dates because they are brilliant and funny and fun to be around—who liberated me from the dull bubble of Long Island every weekend and took my friends and me record shopping on St. Mark's and book browsing at Strand; who brought me to so many Broadway and off-Broadway and off-off-off-Broadway shows that when I tried to tally them at ten years old I already couldn't (and not because I was bad at math but because I'd lost track). I have parents who gave their kid who was born with a really rare disorder a completely normal, regular-in-a-good-way life in which she played sports and had friends and smoked and drank and dyed her hair every color Manic Panic made and did most of the things you're supposed to do when you're growing up. They did not pressure me to find a mate. They did not suggest I choose a more practical profession. They ask with true curiosity about my friends and my job and my writing and my life in general. They are not the parents I had when I was young—who I am able to realize now were just trying to make ends meet and navigate the rocky terrain of blending a family and hold on while my father launched his business. The change was gradual. And yes, in some ways, what had been an obsession with each other changed into an obsession with me. It is very hard to remember—*really* remember—that there was a time I felt insignificant to my parents.

My mom and I still clash sometimes—I'm not sure clashing is a thing mothers and daughters ever grow out of—but it is so different now. If she tells me she doesn't like my lipstick or gives me advice when I haven't asked for it or mentions the fat content in a particular food I'm about to eat, I roll my eyes but do not feel ancient resentments flaring. Or maybe I do, but they don't last very long. In that way, we are the most average. We are just like any other mother and daughter. Mostly I just love her and appreciate that you also can't spell "amazing" or "human" without "ma."

# 5.

## Dieting Will Ruin Your Life

was absolutely lit when I stepped onto the scale. "Down a tenth of a pound," the Weigher Lady told me as she slid the tracker back, and I said "thankthsss" with a big bloody smile.

Weigh-in day happened to coincide with wisdom-teeth-taking-out day, so here I was, at a strip mall WeightWatchers on Long Island with a mouth full of blood-soaked cotton, high on nitrous and a tenth of a pound lighter than the week before. Even stoned I understood that I had done good. Or, I had done okay. I could have done better, always. But at least I didn't do worse.

I was twenty-six years old. After months (years?) on WeightWatchers—time got fuzzy and elastic when I started dieting—I no longer measured my life in midnights and cups of coffee, I measured it in Points and tenths of a pound. Well, in some ways I measured it in cups of coffee: one Point if I took it with skim or CoffeeMate, two if I allowed myself the indulgence of 2 percent, which I almost never did.

The first tipoff that I was worthy that week, which I could tell even in my altered state, was that Weigher Lady had announced the result. When you're up instead of down, they just slide your booklet back to you silently. Sometimes they try not to look you in the eye. Today, though, I was a winner!

A tenth of a pound could have been the two now pulverized teeth I no longer had; it could have been a variable in scale calibration, since I usually went to the gay temple just off Union Square. Most of us in the cult of WeightWatchers tried not to deviate from the scale of our original weigh-in. But faced with the choice of a new scale or no weigh-in at all, I chose the road less traveled (by people who are not completely insane) and had my mother drive me straight from the oral surgeon's office.

My sanguine mouth did not fluster Weigher Lady. These Weigher Ladies and occasional Gentlemen saw a lot: women stripping down to their undies before boarding the scale or arguing about their weekly results as if employees had the power to change physics. Nothing could have stopped those desperate for good news: "I was just shot in the head but I wanted to pop by before calling 911." "I was abducted but I told the nice kidnapper man it was WW day and he said we could stop here first." Honestly? I can imagine it.

Weigher Ladies could determine your mood. They decided whether you were a good or a bad person. Once, a Weigher Lady told me I had gained seven pounds since the week before and I immediately canceled the date I had scheduled for that night, a third one, because I could not conceive of going out with a man who had last seen me when I was possibly seven pounds lighter. Another time, another Weigher Lady told me, "I don't know where you keep it!" and she meant that she could not square the number on the scale with what she saw in front of her. It was a compliment ("You don't look as fat as you are!"), and I took it that way.

When I was little, Dr. Leitch told my mother, who told me, that K-T might account for, at most, six pounds of extra weight. I understood the revelation to be some combination of a warning and a chastisement and a "not so fast" and a "just in case you had any ideas." It meant there was no blaming my size on my congenital disorder. It meant that while, yes, one defect in my appearance was for the most part out of my control, the other was not, and it was my responsibility to *take* control and change it.

My deformity was of utmost concern from the very beginning, but so was my weight. The people around me were so consistently concerned about it, you'd think it was *their* weight. My apparent obesity (a word I no longer use[*]), conflated with a disorder that on its face also looks like an issue of fat, meant

---

[*] The word "obesity" equates fatness with a medical issue and therefore something to be fixed or cured, which folks in the fat-liberation community (I think rightly) believe is a harmful view. The only time I've self-identified as "obese" is when it has given me an advantage, like to get my Covid vaccine in an early round. Thanks, fatphobia!

that even if I could have mastered weight loss (I couldn't, practically nobody can), I would have still been inadequate.

I also couldn't have imagined not wanting to not be fat, even when it felt like an impossibility. Striving to lose weight seemed natural in every sense. What's funny (maybe not "ha-ha" funny) is that for those of us who were gifted the curse of dieting as kids, the size we thought was an inevitability wasn't. We were told we were fat and as a result we were put on diets; those diets broke our relationships to food, which ultimately made most of us fat. Some of us would have been fat anyway, because some bodies are naturally fat the same way others are naturally thin, but we were wrong about our origin stories. We were tampered with, and our reward was becoming the thing people around us were so terrified we would. O. Henry could have written a story about us.

My parents were admirably concerned with social justice and anti-racism decades before I knew what those things meant but drew the line at fat acceptance. My mother founded and ran the high school's Anti-Bias Task Force, and racism was anathema to my dad. A proud but not unique moment I remember vividly is the day he told a family friend, who had just uttered the word "schvartze" in our living room, that he would no longer be welcome in our home if he ever repeated it. I was politically aware and activated from a young age, because I was growing up with liberal Bronx-bred parents who boycotted and blacklisted everything from Nestlé to Wagner in a town of Republican Jews who flaunted Chanel C's even though Coco was a Nazi. Abortion rights were my most passionate cause. I wore a Becky Bell bracelet in high school in honor of the seventeen-year-old who died from sepsis after an illegal abortion in a parental-consent state. It didn't occur to me then, but does now, that it's no coincidence issues of body autonomy are so important to me. My parents supported this streak in me, as they did all my other political interests.

But there was no consciousness-raising about fat dignity or liberation, and there was nothing to be admired about forsaking diet culture. Both of my parents dieted. Being fat was bad. I was fat or on my way there, and I understood that through casual sanctions: junky cereal once a year as a treat, no sweets in the house except for packs of powdered Swiss Miss lite, which I would eat dry with a spoon.

My pediatricians, Drs. Liebman and Mahler, had always been troubled by my weight, but it wasn't until Dr. Leitch said weight loss could make liposuction more effective that something clicked into place for my family: I was *duty-bound* to diet. If I was going to take the drastic step of having surgery (and I was, I had no choice), the least I could do was try to make it a little easier. My prize for this realization was that first Weight-Watchers membership, and I disinterestedly attended meetings with my friend Stacy and her mom, Sandy. (I can't imagine how that first phone call went, my mother saying what translated to, "I'm too thin to need WeightWatchers—can she tag along with you guys?") During our weekly meetings at Temple Hillel, Stacy, Sandy, and I would weigh in like cattle, then sit through a gathering of mostly adult women sharing stories of success (loss!) and heartache (gain). At the end, we'd wish one another a good week (of deprivation, of not eating things we wanted to), the way I imagine alcoholics doing at the end of AA meetings.

That first membership didn't last long because I had no desire to eat less or "better." Nothing about it appealed to me. It was a pointless exercise, so eventually I was allowed to stop. My mother knew I could not be forced to do something I wasn't genuinely interested in. I'm not sure why she ever thought this would be different.

Even though I didn't have it in me to diet, I did come to believe that thin was good and fat was bad, and by extension, foods that *made* you fat were bad. When I went to After-School Program in elementary, my mom gave the staff explicit instructions that I could not have the same snack as everyone else unless it was pretzels. School lunch came with a side of cucumber slices, not those mini packs of chips that were popular. Lunchables, a new product and therefore ubiquitous in the school cafeteria, were absolutely forbidden. Some ingredients and condiments—butter, mayo, lard—were never to be consumed, with the exception of mayonnaise in tuna salad, in which case just a dollop (and the low-fat kind once that was invented). I did not taste an avocado—so much fat stuffed into that little green nub—until my twenties. Same goes for hearts of palm, which have basically zero calories but for some reason my mom thought were filled with fat. I'm guessing she glanced at a can of them once and saw the fat content of the oil they were packed in, then exiled them from our lives without further investigation. Better safe than sorry.

Growing up, even eating too much of a "good" food was

looked down upon. None of the doors in our house had locks, and my mom once walked into the bathroom to find me sitting on the floor eating the end of a baguette I had torn off and run with. (The world hadn't come to view carbs as an enemy yet, so we did keep bread in the house.) Since I knew I'd be chastised eating it out in the open, I had gone into the room where we showered and pissed and shit to do it in secret. When my mom found me, a look of deep disappointment shaded her face and she told me I was disgusting. I held on to that, think about it now sometimes when I'm eating, no matter what I'm eating— *You're disgusting,* just softly to myself—but it didn't make me want to eat any less.

In addition to WeightWatchers, I belonged to numerous gyms throughout my youth and adolescence, the first being Lucille Roberts in Hewlett, where an instructor wrapped in shiny neon spandex gave us a tour of the club the day we joined. When we got to the hip adductor machine, my mother said, "Her right leg is bigger than her left," I'm not sure why, to which the very kind, I'm sure befuddled instructor responded, "Then just do more reps on the right."

By high school I knew that there were two groups of women: the heavy (ponderous, too much while also somehow not enough) and the light (fairy floss girls with limbs like taffy, who were gauzy and diaphanous and practically not even there, whom the boys could pick up without wincing and throw over a shoulder like a prize, because they were).

Starvation was even more pervasive than plastic surgery in my town, the end result for many of my classmates being a stay at the Long Island Jewish eating disorders clinic. Some came up with more creative ways to keep calories down, like chewing their food but not swallowing it, or subsisting on fat-free candy like Blow Pops and gummy worms. Heather Martin, a little bitch who in elementary school once called me a fat pig, was a gummy worm girl. She came back to school the summer after freshman year with a new nose, a new boyfriend, and a new eating disorder. My misanthropic heart filled with joy the day our tenth-grade bio teacher informed us that semen is not fat-free, and I saw the blood drain from Heather's anorexic face.

Though I wanted to be thinner, I didn't take any decisive steps to bring myself closer to that goal. It seemed pointless; I could never compete with the Heather Martins, who were already very thin even before they decided to give up eating. That meant I had it in me to reject dieting. But first, like so many women, I eventually accepted it. Welcomed it. *Rejoiced* in it. The passion with which I refused to diet as a kid finally flipped, and boy oh boy, did I take to it as an adult.

There was nothing remarkable about what finally pushed me into the legions of willing dieters in my twenties: I was fat; I had never really set my mind to dieting; I figured I might as well try. If there was any catalyst, it was the wedding of my college roommate Lauren. When I went to my bridesmaid-dress fitting, hearing my measurements caught me off guard and I thought, *Maybe I'll try dieting.*

I think I was just worn down: *Why not try starving myself? What harm could it do?*

I dieted during a deprived decade spanning ages twenty-six

through thirty-eight, with only brief, unplanned breaks, when I fell off the wagon (meaning, I ate). During those twelve years, dieting was the organizing principle of my life. It was the least interesting but most consistent thing about me.

At first, dieting was a warm hug: It held and stabilized me. Eventually, it felt more like a stranglehold, fixing me in its grip and choking the life out of me. But when it did, I told myself that it was my fault. I am claustrophobic after all; it makes sense that I would want to run. I did, sometimes, but I always came crawling back.

The embrace was, at its base, routine. Repetition. Sameness. It grounded me. I had never before tried to control what I ate, so the order it brought that first time was weirdly sustaining. I'd lost weight only once before, accidentally, when I got to college: While everyone else put on the freshman fifteen, I took it off because I refused to eat in front of strangers.

All those years I was forced to diet as a kid, I literally never, not once, gave it my all or even part of my all. I did not want to diet, so I couldn't. At twenty-six, because I had made the decision myself, because I suddenly found the idea of shrinking interesting, I gave it everything. I chose WeightWatchers because it was at least vaguely familiar, and I knew myself well enough to know that any diet requiring me to eat prepackaged food or substitute smoothies for actual meals would never stick. I wanted to give myself a fighting chance.

When I restarted WeightWatchers as an adult, I was excited by how many options there were—I could eat whatever I wanted! It was just about portion control!—and I experimented, dabbling in the different corners of how to make a diet[*] work. I needed to figure out whether I was someone who wanted to spend my daily twenty-something Points allotment on a few big-ticket items paced smartly throughout the day, letting the fat and protein fill me up, or someone who needed to be grazing always, never not eating, populating the day with an endless stream of low-Points foods designed to distract me from the fact that I was starving.

I very quickly learned that I am the second type of person—I would take a gallon of frozen yogurt made with a sweetener guaranteed to make me shit my pants (reverse Points) over a neat little pastry—and on WeightWatchers, that's okay! If you have a party coming up, for example, though WW will not officially condone it, you can eat only free veggies all day (snack on jicama, it's packed with water!), spend all your Points on liquor, and technically be sticking to your diet lifestyle. I had many WeightWatchers trackers wherein entire days said, "Apple: 0; Wine: 20," which was five four-ounce glasses, in case you're wondering.

I felt like I finally understood nutrition. Because my instincts around food had been broken so early, I had two natural modes when it came to eating: starving or so full I felt sick. There was no in between. Once I let WeightWatchers guide me, I understood its portion recommendations and Points allotments to mean that this was how much normal people ate. I was proud to finally be a normal person who ate normally, even

---

[*] WeightWatchers and other plans like it are adamant that we not call them diets. They are lifestyle changes! They are plans that work for you, not the other way around.

if I was hungry. "Do you want to grab some food?" a guy I was dating once asked at the beginning of my WeightWatchers time, and I said, "No, I had a tablespoon of peanut butter before I left the house." He laughed, but I didn't know I was being funny: I assumed that normal people with normal behaviors around food would find a tablespoon of peanut butter sustaining. WeightWatchers relegated Points to peanut butter per the tablespoon; I had had one; therefore, I was not—or should not be—hungry. I was like a very excited new cult member.

My dedication to the cult made me lose twenty pounds in about fifteen weeks that first stretch. There is nothing like the first time if you're giving it your all, and I do mean all, as in everything: your time, your energy, your focus, your happiness. Because your body has never before been in need, never been deprived when it's in a state of wanting, it will respond like a champ.

The first time you diet, it will be so shockingly easy that you'll wonder why you resisted for so long—nobody had told you how easy it would be. Sure, sometimes you feel hungry and yes, life is a little bit less fun, but you are getting *thin,* and *nothing tastes as good as thin feels.*

There are lies there. Loads of things taste as good—better!—than thin feels. There is no accurate conversion chart for the two. It makes no sense. But it's impossible to get talked into dieting without somebody lying to you. All I knew was that for the first time in my life, I was shrinking because of a conscious decision to do so. I felt powerful.

The compliments I got from friends and family after that initial loss were overwhelming, and I don't mean the ones that told me how great I looked, though I liked those, too. No, the ones that meant the most were the suggestions that I was somehow now a better person. I was strong; I was dedicated; I was *brave*. Keeping the weight off was as important to the people around me as it was to me—maybe even more important!—and I owed it to them not to disappoint.

Except, I did disappoint, because the pounds (and then some) came back, so I had to start again. And then I had to start again, again. Nobody tells you that every successive attempt to diet after that first time will be harder and bring fewer returns. With every shameful trip back to WeightWatchers—a hanging head, a fresh booklet, something like an apology to the Weigher Lady—came a new and more restrictive way of eating, and in this way, WeightWatchers lived up to its promise: It *did* become a lifestyle. It became the thing I maneuvered everything else in my life around. It was the on-again, off-again relationship I could not shake.

A couple of years into WeightWatchers, I had a very strict routine. Every morning I woke up and put a teapot on the stove to make coffee from my French press, then took a quick shower timed to end just as the kettle whistled. I allowed myself two cups of coffee, with one tablespoon of liquid low-fat Coffee-Mate in each. As my hair dried, I made a three-egg-white omelet with one WeightWatchers string cheese and a dollop of salsa, plus two slices of WeightWatchers bread with spray butter. Occasionally I allowed myself a fourth egg white, but only if I was very hungry. For a mid-morning snack, I'd pack an apple or a bag of baby carrots—sometimes an entire bag, the big one, and I would eat nearly the whole thing—and hope that work would be so busy, I wouldn't be able to have lunch until around four P.M. I drank gallons of water, diet soda, and tea throughout the day to keep myself feeling full, even though tea sort of nauseates me. I liked that its built-in sickness-making quality could dampen my hunger. Lunch was either zero-Points Weight-Watchers soup, a small sweet potato, a salad with nonfat dressing, or a peanut butter sandwich on WeightWatchers bread. Dinner was six Trader Joe's soy nuggets with as much mustard as I wanted and a tablespoon of ketchup to keep it in the zero-Points range. (WeightWatchers alchemy could convert too much of a zero-Points food into a one-Point food, so you had to be careful.) I tried to wait as long as I could to eat dinner so that I didn't need a snack afterward, but if I did, it'd be a Weight-Watchers ice cream bar or maybe twenty dark chocolate–covered soybeans from Trader Joe's. Each one was the size of a fat grain of rice, and I counted them out on my bed.

Those were just the weekdays. Weekends were much, much harder.

Dieting is easier if there are other things in your life that feel unsteady or chaotic or unsafe. For example, I began what would become my most successful go at WeightWatchers right after starting a new job and having a really terrible boyfriend (the one with the cat) move in. I was so anxious at work and so uncomfortable at home, food control became the only stable force in my life. The steps I needed to take to keep starving myself became the hug. Looking forward to the ten A.M. apple, cutting the vegetables for the zero-Points soup, trying to eat a low-fat cookie as slowly as possible, chewing it down to gravel and trying to feel it drip into my empty stomach—all hugs. Not bear hugs anymore, maybe; bony ones, all corners and elbows.

It's a sensitive seesaw, though, because dieting is harder if there is *nothing* in your life that is currently bringing you joy. If you are, for example, coming off the heels of a pandemic and feeling a sort of post-traumatic shock, but you've already pulled your other joy levers (like online shopping, which has left you with a massive credit card bill you can't pay off), and the only thing that still gives you a little jolt of excitement is food, trying to diet now will be incredibly hard, because eating is the last source of happiness you have, and it doesn't even make you that happy anymore, but at least it's something.

Weight loss causes an identity crisis for anyone who accomplishes it. Hearing that you look great makes you wonder what they thought you looked like before. Being congratulated for your willpower and stick-to-it-ness against the enemies of hunger and need teaches you that denying your instincts is important, and that discomfort—in the form of hunger pains, light-headedness, obsessiveness—are signs of success.

For me, dieting caused a two-pronged identity crisis or maybe an identity crisis superimposed on another one. My deformity and fatness had always been conflated, so being told I looked thin was the same as being told I looked normal, even though I didn't. Weight loss put even more distance between me and my body.

My mental health was a mess when I was dieting. Here's why.

## Things That Happen While You're in Pursuit of a Weight-Loss Goal

—When you hit your goal on a diet, you inherit a new one: maintaining. Gaining weight is easy. Losing weight can be easy. Keeping weight off—that is, staying the same weight—is very, very hard, especially when you're trying.

—You will body check, meaning you will become obsessed with mirrors and other reflective surfaces—anything that can answer the question of what you look like and by extension whether you are good. One of my most pervasive forms of body checking was running my fingers up and down my chin while eating anything bad (potato chips, chocolate), trying to ward off a nascent double chin.

—You will become an irritating friend, constantly asking those closest to you to affirm that you do not look fatter than you did a month, a day, a minute ago. You will be aware of how annoying you are but will be powerless to stop.

—You will become addicted to math, even if you hate math. Instead of counting sheep, you will retell yourself the story of your Points that day, checking and rechecking them, as a way to lull yourself into an anxious slumber and get as quickly as you can to another day of not eating.

—You will become joyless. Well, first you'll become joyful, riding that high of finally or again being thin (and therefore good), and that euphoria will carry you for a time. But then, in order to sustain that euphoria, you will need to excise all joy from your life, and ironically, you will do this joyfully. You will say no to parties. Sometimes you'll say yes to parties, but you'll eat first. Sometimes you'll say yes to parties and instead of eating first you will starve yourself all day so you can eat there. Sometimes you'll say yes to parties and instead of eating at all, you'll use all your Points on alcohol. Sometimes you'll drink so much that you'll throw up, and you will feel relieved. Damage undone. Mischief managed.

—You will defy your instincts. Are you hungry? Too bad. Can't ignore it? Have an apple. Can't afford it? Drink some water. (Fruit is free on WeightWatchers now, but it wasn't always.)

—If you're me, you'll go on a beach vacation and relax not in the sand or at the pool but by repeatedly counting the days until you're home, looking forward to a WeightWatchers meeting the way you should have looked forward to the vacation. Maybe once you're home you'll be so desperate for a check-in that you'll arrive before the center has opened and sit on the sidewalk, a jangle of nerves waiting for someone to arrive, unlock the doors, and weigh you. (Little You, who dreaded doctors' appointments months in advance because of the prospect of the scale, did not see this coming.) If it turns out you have stayed the same or perhaps even lost a pound, you will decide you had a good vacation.

—You will have weeks that, for reasons you can't understand (you were perfect! You said no to everything!), you gain. The person weighing you will not say, "It's okay, you can't just lose week after week, that's not normal or realistic for a body." You will vow to be *even more perfect,* meaning you will vow to eat less.

—You will give yourself a cheat day because the ~~diet~~ lifestyle is becoming unsustainable; plus, you've read that calorie loading can jump-start your metabolism. Cheat day will become the best day of the week, the thing you look forward to more than you've ever looked forward to anything. Except that little by little, cheat day will become a sort of desperate binge of whatever you can get into your mouth before midnight, when you turn into a pumpkin. (Pumpkin has zero Points, btw.) You will gorge yourself on whatever you can, eating too much, drinking too much, trying to make yourself so stuffed and complete that maybe the first few days of the coming week won't feel so desperate. Maybe you'll be too sick to eat at all.

—You. Will. Poofie.* If you diet like I did—by keeping yourself perpetually full on a giant intake of cruciferous veggies— you will poofie all the time. You will be unable to stop the poofies from happening and will live in perpetual fear that you will poofie during a meeting or on a date or at the gynecologist or in bed, and you will. You will sometimes walk down the street with a steady soundtrack of poofies, so that you are a one-woman walking Philip Glass production, each footstep a poison staccato. Maybe once when you're about to have drunken

---

* Though we cursed freely in my house growing up, one word that was absolutely, unequivocally banned was "fart." It's hard for me to even type it. We called farts "poofies." The verb form is "to poofie." Pronunciation-wise, its first syllable rhymes with the French word for egg, *oeuf,* or the English word "hoof," not the longer double *oo* of "roof" or "stoop." Feel free to use it. If this book accomplishes nothing else, please let it be that people stop saying "fart."

sex with a friend, as you feel the pressure of his cock bearing down on you, you'll sense that familiar gurgle rising and push him off you, pretending that you changed your mind because you don't want to jeopardize your friendship, when actually you're just afraid that one thrust of his hips will turn you into a human whoopie cushion.

—You will see other people eating—at restaurants, on Instagram—and wonder how they do it, eating freely, forgetting that you used to eat freely, too; forgetting that not everyone forces herself to steal from tomorrow's breakfast to earn the right to tonight's dinner.

—You will panic when steady weight loss turns to a plateau and eventually to gains, and perhaps your way of managing that panic will be to try to make a fresh start every week, asking the Weigher Lady to reregister you anew, with a clean booklet, so you can start from a literal blank page. You are recommitting, like a born-again Christian does to her lord and savior.

—You will lose your personal sense of style, because now that more things fit, you want whatever you can get onto your body, just to prove that you can. Or maybe it's the reverse, that before, when you were fatter, when fewer things fit, *that* was when you had no personal sense of style. No matter what, you will end up confused.

—You will sort of . . . lose your mind? By which I mean that your brain will cease to work the way it used to and you will become Amelia Bedelia. Maybe you'll go to dinner at a vegan restaurant with your friend Alison and order the battered seitan. When it arrives you will be crestfallen. You thought "battered" meant pounded with a mallet—physically battered—not dipped in batter and then fried. Because it was your mistake, you will not send it back; instead, you will move your seitan around the plate but not actually eat it and be grateful for the opportunity to skip a meal without looking like you meant to.

—You will (of course) sometimes fail at sticking to your strict lifestyle plan, and the result will be a binge. The joke will be on you, because eating doesn't even feel good anymore. The foods you pined for when dieting hold no thrill once you actually have them, and in this way, you have robbed yourself of the one thing you started with: a love of food. Binges will sit like a boulder in your body, feeling cumbersome and foreign, tethering you to a sadistic netherworld where, okay, fine, you

Salsa
W.W. bread
Salsa

`a re-creation of a recently unearthed grocery list from the time when I lost my mind. (I was merely scatterbrained, not planning on salsa sandwiches.)

can eat, but you cannot enjoy it. You will think that you deserve this, for you are weak.

—You will have the exact same thing for dinner every night for a period of six straight months because you are terrified of what will happen if you introduce something new, not realizing that you've developed something called orthorexia. Any suggestion that you deviate from your regular menu will terrify you, even if the number on the scale is not budging. You will honestly believe that what you are doing is healthy, that it was all those other years when you didn't do this that you were sick.

—Maybe, as editor in chief of *Time Out New York,* you will be tapped to cover the fifty best dishes in New York for local TV. As you sit at a table other people must book a month in advance, laden with free food, you will sheepishly ask the director just before she rolls, "Do I have to actually take a bite?" When she says it's up to you, you opt instead to hold your fork aloft, as if it were on its way to your mouth, while smiling and laughing at everything the thin show host says, then place the fork down again, and your smile and laugh will be real because you are so relieved that you were not forced to eat.

—You will dread holidays you used to look forward to, like Thanksgiving. (If observing the world's most anxious people sounds like your cup of zero-Points tea, pop into your local WeightWatchers on the last Tuesday or Wednesday in November.) If you're lucky, fate will intervene, like it did for me years ago, when a table spontaneously collapsed and those of us tending to all the screaming children missed the big feast. In November 2020, years after I purposely stopped monitoring what I ate, I thought about how elated my dieting self would have been for the pandemic, dodging that turkey-shaped bullet and instead getting to sit alone on my couch, thinking that was happiness, a living monument to the new American legacy of deprivation.

—You will try extreme measures, like the HCG diet, on which, for just three thousand dollars, a so-called medical professional will prescribe you human chorionic gonadotropin, fertility hormones that trick your body into thinking you are pregnant and supposedly make you lose weight. The key is sticking to five hundred calories a day for the diet to work. Do that and you are guaranteed to lose a pound a day; if you plateau—a plateau on the HCG diet is when you haven't lost a pound in three days—you will jiggle the handle of your system by eating only six apples or a piece of steak with absolutely nothing on it. You pick your poison. The reward is getting to return to your five hundred calories the next day. Mazel tov.

If you are a naturally thin person—and I mean this—congratulations. Congratulations, because the DNA you inherited that made you thin gave you a tremendous amount of power and privilege in this world. I know it doesn't mean you always love your body and that you never feel insecure. But it also means that doctors likely take you more seriously and don't ascribe every ailment that plagues you (endometriosis, broken toe) to your fatness—though doctors have very far to go when it comes to their willingness and ability to hear *all* women. There is a very narrow acceptable range for us, just a sliver, really, wherein we are neither too fat nor too thin but just right. But if you are thin, even if you are *too* thin, life is inherently safer. You don't worry about the width of seats at the theater. You don't think about the sturdiness of chairs. You haven't been taught that if you did have to worry about any of those things, it would be your fault and your problem to solve. The world order puts thin people at the top, with the rest of us below struggling for air. Many of us have been gasping for decades.

For those of us who were indoctrinated early, there was no hope of evading the chains of diet culture completely; the best-case scenario, one we didn't know existed yet, is the one I ended up in for a time: willfully rejecting the notion that I was duty bound to shrink myself. Let that sink in for a second. We are not required to make ourselves smaller. We do not become better people when we do and therefore do not become worse when we don't. The act of shrinking has no moral charge. It is very, very recently that I started to truly believe that. It happened little by little, the same way diet indoctrination had.

There's a scene in *The West Wing* when press secretary C.J. Cregg, played by Allison Janney, takes a meeting with the Organization of Cartographers for Social Equality, which says that the world map we use, the Mercator projection, drafted in 1569, is incorrect, both in the way it sizes and positions countries. Their solution? A new map that puts the Southern Hemisphere at the top and the Northern Hemisphere at the bottom. "You can't do that," C.J. says. Why not? they ask. "Because it's freaking me out," she replies.

That's what deciding not to diet feels like; or rather, that's what the moment *right before* deciding not to diet feels like if you're someone who has always just accepted the way you think things are: Thin is better, north goes at the top. But those aren't foregone conclusions, and they're not natural or good. We've just been taught that they are, so now we believe it. The reality was always there, true north, only I'd somehow never seen it. It's like how I—a proud liberal, a progressive, an *ally*—never thought to wonder about my Black friends' experiences with police until Black Lives Matter. I never wondered how walking down the street or getting stopped for speeding was different for me. How? *HOW?!?* Once you realize it, the amplitude of your ignorance could—and should—stun you. The world does not look the way you thought it did, and it was always clear; you just never bothered to check, because you didn't have to.

My most successful go at WeightWatchers—if success is measured by pounds lost and nothing else—was my last. I was thirty-eight when it started, years after my wisdom teeth, and I managed to keep off forty pounds for about two years. I don't know what triggered my plateau and reversal; I could never quite pinpoint it, even though it was always inevitable. Practically no one has the resolve, energy, and wherewithal to keep up the tireless effort it takes to diet in perpetuity. The only exception is anyone wealthy and famous enough and so desperate to be thin because their livelihood depends on it that they can outsource the task of control to others: trainers, personal chefs, doctors, whatever the fuck an accountability coach is.

Once I started to put the forty pounds back on, I told myself it was okay, that I knew this was coming and as long as my clothes fit, I had nothing to worry about.

When my clothes no longer fit, I told myself that I would lean into eating for a while and then, like all the other times, start to diet again.

When I found myself fatter than I'd ever been in my life, I told myself that this, too, was part of the reality of dieting—each time you gain weight back, you tend to gain more of it—but I'd successfully dieted before and could successfully diet again. It was a process I'd endured and assumed I would endure for the rest of my life: lose, gain, restart. Only, this time, something was different. I couldn't get myself back to WeightWatchers, no matter how hard I tried. I would set a day-before alert in my phone and every time it went off move it back a week.

It wasn't new that I didn't want to go back, but what happened next was: I realized that I didn't *have to*.

I did not have to go back to WeightWatchers. I can't explain how revolutionary this was.

I didn't think about or understand the ramifications of the decision—my clothes would keep not fitting, I'd need to see a nutritional therapist to help me learn intuitive eating, which is what comes naturally to anyone who wasn't tampered with.

I didn't want to be fat, but I didn't want to diet even more than I didn't want to be fat, so I wouldn't. Dieting had worn me out. I cannot tell you what the final straw was, but I was done. The decision to give up dieting was probably the first decision, after giving up surgery, that I made about my body that was for me and me alone.

As time went on after my deprogramming from the cult of WeightWatchers, my body became fatter, weirder, slower, softer. Kicking diet culture didn't mean I always loved what I saw in the mirror or in photos. It didn't mean I never fat-shamed myself. All it meant, on its best days, was an absence of the rumination I'd come to believe was my forever fate. It meant I didn't lie in bed at night counting Points and didn't cancel plans with people I love because of a fear that I would lose control and eat. It meant I ate!

Sometimes even in my deprogramming years I'd catch myself uttering that old familiar mantra under my breath while I was eating: "You're disgusting, you're disgusting, you're disgusting." It didn't even matter what I was eating—the pure act of ingestion was such an enemy for so long that this credo could rear its head without warning.

A familiar refrain to dieters eager for things to go faster is that it took a long time to put on the weight, so it only makes sense that patience is required to take it off. This rare bit of kindness in the diet world can be applied to deprogramming, too: It took a lifetime to accept and embody the supposed norms and strictures of judgment, denial, and shame, so it takes some time to unlearn it. Deprogramming from any cult is an arduous journey made up of many baby steps, and this one is no exception. Diet Culture is the umbrella cult; WeightWatchers is merely a sect, alongside Noom, Jenny Craig, Nutrisystem, HCG, South Beach, Bloat Be Gone, Starvation Nation, Puke-o-Rama. (I made up those last three, but they could be real, right?) The sects reel you in and keep you with different tactics, but in the end, they are all the same, with the same instructions: *Eat less.* An injection of HCG may give you that extra little boost you need, like the motor on a CitiBike when you're struggling up a hill, but the thing getting the result is always deprivation. In the Choose Your Own Adventure that is dieting, the catch is that no matter which path you pick, you end up in the same place, which makes it less of an adventure and more like a trap. When I left WeightWatchers, I decided to choose something else.

For a little while at least.

## *2023, Forty-Six Years Old*

The Ozempic Era has been a doozy for those of us on a path of actively disengaging from diet culture and engaging with fat liberation. After eight years of quietly gaining a number of pounds I could not quantify because I no longer weighed myself, after years of experiencing an absence of fear around food, without really stopping to think about what I was doing or why I was doing it, I made an appointment with my doctor to talk about Ozempic. I hadn't even *remotely* been thinking about trying to lose weight when it happened, then suddenly I was. How could I not be, I guess: There was an omnipresent inundation of suddenly shrunken celebrities and whispers of how they'd gotten so small so fast. Even the thought of considering it made me feel guilty and ashamed and traitorous, but I couldn't resist. *What harm could it do?* I missed my cheekbones. I missed being able to see my bikini line when I shaved. Maybe I wouldn't feel like I was dragging myself around so much. Maybe the subway stairs wouldn't seem so daunting.

I didn't need to get super skinny. Maybe I wouldn't even change what I ate! I'd just inject the drug and see what happened, and if the answer was nothing, then fine. Ideologically, nothing would have to change for me because nothing had really changed ever. Even after I left WeightWatchers, even when I was living without constant surveillance of what entered my mouth, despite everything I believed intellectually and for other people, I always would have preferred to be thinner. That's hard to admit, but it's true.

I think that's partly because even in the world of fat positivity, I have felt on the outskirts. When I see photos of Lizzo and Beth Ditto and Paloma Elsesser and Tess Holliday and Bridget Everett and Melissa McCarthy with their plump bellies and beautiful rolls of fat falling symmetrically everywhere, I do not see myself. When I look at them I see pretty women who are fat. When I look at myself I see a woman who has the potential to be pretty if not for the amorphous blob of fatness that results in a side profile I can only describe as Asymmetric Penguin. I would be okay being fat if I were a beautiful fat woman, but I am not, I tell myself. And as much as I hate dieting and diet culture, I spent too long being told that I was too big to not still wish I were small.

After that first wave of Ozempic guilt—just from a phone call—a fear crept in. If I took the drug, I knew I would become obsessive. I would eventually have to learn to love myself all over again, because if dieting has taught me anything, it's that you cannot put a pin in a feeling you once had, like self-acceptance, and save it for later. I would ruin my life all over again, just for a few months of maybe getting a little skinnier. I would ruin my life and also suffer whatever as-yet-undiscovered (or undisclosed) dangers the drugs bring. I would ruin my life and on top of that feel guilty because how can I be a person who talks about the evils of dieting while sort of dieting?

The call with my doctor marked the first time in a long time that I'd had a conversation about my size, and even longer since I'd heard someone refer to it as a medical condition. My doctor, who has always abided my instructions not to tell me my weight, warned that going on Ozempic or another semaglutide would mean *having* to know my weight so she could document it for my insurance company. But she wasn't trying to talk me out of it. She seemed excited, actually. She thought this class of drug, particularly Wegovy, could be a great solution to the problem of my weight, which I hadn't thought of as a problem in a very long time. I was, for once, making a doctor happy on the topic of my size by agreeing to explore, at least verbally, options to remedy my fatness. Just my contemplation of falling (no, jumping) off the wagon felt like a transgression, only, here was a medical professional encouraging me to do it. *Jump!* Now I didn't even know what the wagon was. Was it dieting or not dieting? I was astounded by how quickly I became disoriented.

There were land mines in our conversation my doctor didn't know were there: "Would I have to diet?" I asked her. "No," she said, "just, you know, eat healthy." The person who'd prescribed me HCG years before had said something similarly dismissive: "It's just food," like, no big deal. (Nothing has ever resonated with me less.)

What about when I wanted to go off Wegovy—would I get fatter than when I started? No, of course not, my doctor said. But she misunderstood me, because she does not have my history. She answered me literally, scientifically: There was nothing about the drug that could make a person gain back more weight than when she started. But I knew the answer was yes before I asked it. If the point of these drugs was to make me not hungry, and going off them meant returning to hunger, then of course I would gain more, just as I had when diet culture was foisted upon me as a kid and I later broke free.

Right after the appointment, I called Melissa—one of my

very best friends and comrade in anti-dieting—and confessed for the mere contemplation of drugs, as if she were a priest and I had just slept with somebody's husband.

She was bewildered. "Why are you apologizing to *me?*" she asked, and I understood what she meant: It was my body. If anyone deserved an apology right now, it was me, from me, along with my doctors and my parents and society and anyone else who had ever made me feel like it was my duty to shrink.

After the call, after years of eating whatever I wanted, whenever I wanted, I was suddenly more conscious of how much food I was taking in every day. I was more anxious. I was making more thoughtful decisions about what and when I ate and chastising myself just a little anytime I put something in my mouth if I was not sufficiently hungry to do so (whatever that means). To many of you reading this, some of that—the "thoughtful" part especially—may sound positive, but it's not. For me, thoughtful is one step away from obsessive and obsessive is perilously close to disordered.

I was triggered and also stuck in a no-man's land. After just one phone call I had gone from eating with no guilt and being (I thought) relatively neutral about my fatness to self-consciously eating and being critical of and worried about my fatness. I wasn't even taking the fucking drug yet. (Somebody print the "I called my doctor about Wegovy and all I got was this lousy chronic anxiety back" T-shirts.)

Then I decided: *Screw it, if I'm here already, I might as well try.* So I did. I started taking Wegovy.

I ordered a scale and was shocked by the number it revealed when I precariously stepped on that first time. I couldn't stop thinking about the number. And I couldn't stop thinking about how angry I was that I let this happen, and "this" was both "gaining so much weight" *and* "falling back into diet culture." And I couldn't stop thinking about how swiftly my doctor, who I loved for her kindness, went from not talking about my weight at all to remarking during each successive visit how great I was starting to look and how well I was doing! And I couldn't stop marveling at just how quickly I went from being a relatively calm anti-dieter to *PLEASE GOD DON'T LET THESE DRUGS STOP WORKING.*

If you want to be thinner but have no instincts to fall back on, Wegovy becomes the helpful bull's-eye in a Venn diagram of impossible options.

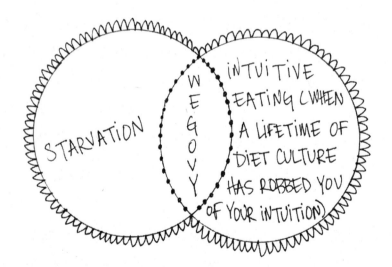

As I write this, I have been taking Wegovy for almost a year. I have lost weight. In the first couple months, I loved how I felt, and mostly I loved what a lot of people on these drugs describe as an absence of food noise. I was eating less, but I was not doing what I did on WeightWatchers all those years, which is track every bite and restrict myself. I ate whatever I wanted, I just got full faster. I felt no guilt or worry or shame or regret. I went on vacations without studying menus ahead of time. I went out with friends and ordered anything I wanted.

I was doing what I'd always hoped to do with intuitive eating post–WeightWatchers but was never quite able to. It wasn't real—how could I be doing something intuitively when there was a literal medicine controlling how much I craved and could hold?—but emotionally, that's what it felt like. At the very beginning of taking Wegovy, I lived in two worlds that had never before overlapped for me: I was sated but it was also incredibly quiet. I imagine it's what people who have never been broken by diet culture feel like naturally. It was miraculous.

Nearly a year in I can't say it's as quiet. Old disordered habits have crept back, and my world has gotten smaller, because calorie restriction is a world shrinker no matter how you do it. I find myself tallying what I've eaten at the end of a day and saying no to things I want to put in my mouth. I find myself eating less and less, on purpose, and getting nervous if I eat (what I decide is) too much. I've worked on this before and I'll probably work on it again. I am still mostly happy. More old clothes fit. I like the way I look in them. I hate to admit that, because a better solution would be that I were not conditioned to think appearing one way in an item of clothing is somehow better than another.

At first I told no one I was taking Wegovy, then I started telling everyone because (as you've probably gathered) I tell everybody everything. Mostly it was a defense: When friends who'd previously watched me clean my plate raised an eyebrow (or I worried that they did) as I pushed away a quarter-eaten meal, I went with humor as confession: "I want to keep eating but I can't because of Wegovy!" If I felt a wave of nausea and left in a hurry, I'd text, "Sorry I ran out of the bar so fast— I drank on an empty stomach because I have disordered eating and now I feel like I'm going to puke, hahahahahahaha." I tried to remember that I didn't owe it to anyone to eat, just as I'd never owed it to anyone not to.

When I hear a thin person groaning about Ozempic and Mounjaro and Wegovy, expressing shock at the idea that people would consider injecting themselves with drugs and enduring headaches, nausea, and constipation all for the potential promise of being thinner, I think, "Oh, fuck off." *Of course* we will. We've been told our whole lives that thinner is the goal above all else. Fuck off, and before you go, thank your lucky stars that nobody's been telling you *your* life may not be worth living if you can't get thinner. Fuck off and be happy that the concept (supposedly) seems so foreign to you.

When a medical doctor wrote a story for *New York Magazine* titled "What if Ozempic Is Just a Good Thing?" and compared semaglutides to Suboxone, which treats opioid addiction, I thought, *FUCK OFF,* even though she made a lot of good points and taught me things I didn't know about the drug I was taking.

Her thesis rested on the idea of what she considers two epidemics: obesity and opioids. They are *not* the same thing, and treating fatness as a disease and normalizing weight-loss injections guarantees there will be future generations of people with eating as disordered as mine. I still think this, even though I inject myself with those drugs. I want better for the younger mes out there who still have a fighting chance.

I believe in fat liberation. I hold both things simultaneously— I want to feel thinner and resent that I want to, but I also resent the fat activists who have added guilt to my plate. A fat-positive influencer I like posted on her Instagram recently that any person actively trying to lose weight is harming fat people, and I thought, *Please fuck all the way off.* Well, first I thought, *Oh god,* and then I thought, *I am the worst,* and *then* I thought, *Wait, actually, please fuck all the way off,* and also, *Maybe don't tell me what to do with my body.*

She's not wrong—*I* am one of the people in a bigger body who I'm harming by taking Wegovy—and I wish I didn't wish to be smaller. I'm not saying I don't feel a pang of cowardice when I talk to friends in the fat-liberation community and purposely avoid the topic—a topic we used to talk about so much— I'm saying that it cannot be on me. Something was done to me. I have paid for it. I am paying for it. I cannot take on the responsibility of caring for this influencer's body over caring for my own. I can try my best to be an ally while working out my own stuff—or not working out my own stuff, because it's really none of her business and I don't actually owe her that, I don't think. Where I have ended up (for now) is not perfect, but then, nothing ever is, and that's another one of the kindnesses

I'm trying to allow myself. Striving to be perfect and inoffensive and pleasant and palatable to all people (except myself) is not something I want to spend my energy on anymore.

It might be different if I had a kid. One of the reasons I'm so glad I don't want children is that I have no idea how I would spare them from disordered eating. I have no idea how I would model a healthy relationship with food for them to follow, because I don't have one. I had one, long ago, before I can remember it, but it was taken from me, left in the bathroom with the crumbs of that baguette.

If I had a child, I would think twice about injecting myself with a drug meant to make me smaller, because I would absolutely not want to send the message—tacitly or overtly—to this growing sponge of a human that she should ever feel pressured to change, and I *certainly* would not want her to contemplate ingesting a very new drug in order to do it. I am more protective of my imaginary offspring than I am of my own body, just as I flinch anytime I hear a parent with a child in earshot talk about having eaten too much or walking off a meal or being upset that their body doesn't look like it used to. "Your kids can hear you," I want to tell them. But that's easy for me to say, because I don't have someone little depending on me to help her build self-worth while I'm still working on my own. And I'm so glad for that.

I have no exit plan. I've done this dance enough times to know it probably won't be my last. Weight loss always feels slippery, and this version of it is the most unctuous, because it was too easy. It does not feel real or like it's mine or that it's sustainable, and it's probably not. Maybe by the time you read this I will no longer be on Wegovy. Maybe I will be on it for life. Is that even an option? Do the doctors know yet? (I told you, I ask very few questions at medical appointments.) I am a lab rat, figuring things out as I go, and if I drop dead because it turns out Wegovy can kill you, like fen-phen and other drugs before it, I suppose I'll have my answer. If that happens, please remember that it was not my fault I ended up where I did, and make sure I wear something cool to my funeral (#coffintalk).

## Drinking Game:
## Spot the Assholes Edition

Recognizing the intrinsic anti-fatness and deformity-aversion of mainstream culture can be tough. We've been conditioned since birth to accept that some bodies are good and others are bad. The best way to measure just how widespread the problem is? A drinking game! Feel free to substitute food for drink if that's your thing. Do both. Or neither. Again, it's your body (not really if you're reading this in the United States, but for our purposes):

- Drink every time you see an ad or commercial for some miracle program or piece of equipment that promises to make you smaller, leaner, tighter, better.

- Drink again if it says it can do it permanently.

- Be sure to include the ones you think are "healthy" (Weight-Watchers, Noom) and the ones that seem questionable (Nutrisystem, Nite Burn), because they are all exactly the same.

- Drink every time people you like disappoint you by revealing themselves to be fatphobic; e.g., Emily Blunt regales a talk show host with a story whose punch line hinges on the fat-shaming of a waitress; Anderson Cooper refers to Donald Trump as "an obese turtle on his back flailing in the hot sun" when there are so many worthier things to call him (racist, rapist, psychopath, shit-filled skin tag).

- Drink every time a TV show you like with a message of inclusion (say, *Will & Grace*) marginalizes an outsider body, which, sure, serves as a referendum on the shallowness of the character, but also elicits a cheap laugh and makes you wonder how you would feel if you were the butt of the joke (e.g., Grace is skeeved out by a boyfriend with six toes in the episode "Three's a Crowd, Six Is a Freak Show").

- Drink every time you see an ad, Instagram tutorial, or vlog encouraging you to alter the way you look (whether by facial contouring, camera angling, or otherwise).

- Drink every time you feel guilty about putting something in your mouth.

- Drink again if you just thought, *That's what she said,* because food, hunger, and sexual signaling are actually linked—you're not imagining it.

- Drink anytime you hear a celebrity or influencer who is talking about weight loss make a point to say they don't care what people look like, they just want everyone to be *healthy.*

- Drink again if you wonder why they care so much that people are healthy.

- Drink again if you think it's weird how much they supposedly care that people are healthy but aren't outspoken when it comes to issues like food insecurity and affordable housing and environmental racism and wealth distribution and medical access and gun control because wouldn't working on those issues be a better way to make sure people are healthy than trying to get them to work out or diet?

- Drink anytime society congratulates itself for accepting someone in a "bigger" body, who you know is not really big at all but merely has bodacious boobs and/or is simply not emaciated (e.g., Kate Upton, Iskra Lawrence).

- Drink anytime a character is revealed to have a "flaw" that is meant to humanize her but is so negligible that it only highlights the limitations of what we'll accept as flaws. Example: In the *Sex and the City* episode "The Freak Show" (sensing a theme?), Carrie and her guy swap imperfections. His? A tattoo of Tweety Bird gotten while drunk at a bachelor party. "What about you?" he asks. "You're probably perfect." "No," she says, coyly pointing to a *half-inch scar* on her knee. "Three stitches. I got into a fight with a third-grade bully."

- Drink anytime you realize that mainstream standards of "beauty" are mostly standards of "whiteness."

- Drink anytime a supposedly (or implicitly) feminist podcast you're listening to features the hosts reading ads for diet products.

- Drink anytime anyone receives accolades for weight loss, as if they have done something morally good or beneficial to society as opposed to what they have actually done, which is get smaller.

- Drink anytime someone you thought of as an ally (like me?) inspires disappointment, pity, or anger because she has regressed in her anti-diet journey.

- Drink again if the reason you find this upsetting is because it means you could also regress.

- Drink every time you watch a dating show that claims to match people based on more than physical attraction (*Love Is Blind, Married at First Sight*) yet for some reason features almost exclusively contestants who are thin, able-bodied, and without deformities.

- Drink once for every fictional character you can think of who has a backstory that involves a time when they were fat and therefore uncool. Drink again if flashbacks include the thin actor who plays that character wearing a fat suit (two freebies to get you started: Courteney Cox on *Friends,* Max Greenfield on *New Girl*).

- Drink every time you come upon the particularly infuriating and misogynistic trope of men wanting women to be thin but without trying. Example: Writer Brad Falchuk, in wishing his wife, Gwyneth Paltrow, a happy birthday on Instagram, marvels at the fact that she "drinks whiskey and eats fried food yet still manages to look like that," as if it weren't hard enough to look like *that* (willowy, blonde, fair, muscular in only the right spots), we now also have to seem effortless about it, so as not to turn off men with the burden of our labor. (Side note: *Is* that how she eats? Because I'm pretty sure I just watched a video in which she said she has bone broth for lunch every day.)

- And while we're here, drink every time you encounter someone who is trying very hard to convince you that "intermittent fasting" or "orthorexia" or "starvation" is something called "wellness."

- Drink every time someone you love, who loves you, comments on your body, even positively.

- Stop for a second to think about whether it was really positive or just seemed that way; e.g., "You look great! Did you lose weight?" which a) insinuates you were somehow inadequate before, and b) equates looking good with being thin. Drink if a or b apply.

- Drink even if a and b don't apply, because commenting on someone's body for any reason at all, unless implicitly asked, is (we've been over this) not okay.

- Drink anytime a celebrity (like Elizabeth Hurley) says something cruelly disparaging about another celebrity in a magazine (*Allure,* 2000) along the lines of "I've always thought Marilyn Monroe looked fabulous, but I'd kill myself if I was that fat," leading you to wonder, *What would that shallow cunt do if she had* my *body? Kill herself* twice?

- Drink anytime someone famous is accused of losing weight with help from bariatric surgery and/or drugs and feigns (or truly feels) offense, e.g., Jesse Plemons tells the *Los Angeles Times,* "It's really unfortunate that I decided to get healthy when everyone decided to take Ozempic. It doesn't matter. Everyone's going to think I took Ozempic anyways."

- Drink again when that person insists that he put in the real, hard work of diet and exercise and did not take any shortcuts, as if one way of losing weight is more commendable than another, as if people don't have enough to worry about without competing over whose chosen method of disappearing is most virtuous instead of wondering why we—and women especially—so enthusiastically participate in our own disappearance in the first place.

- Drink when you realize that an entire group of people—fat people—are routinely implored and encouraged by doctors to take those "shortcuts" and denied care if they refuse.

- Drink anytime a group of very thin women expresses worry about a member of their circle who has gotten *too* thin (start with any *Real Housewives* franchise populated by mostly white women).

- Drink if you can't think of one work of literature, theater, television, or film that features a character with a physical deformity that doesn't define their entire being.

- Or make them saintly.

- Or fiendish.

- Drink anytime a movie or TV show employs a physical deformity to imbue a character with magic.

- Or meaning.

- Or as a juxtaposition to the character's beautiful interior.

- Drink when you realize you've drunk so much you feel sick, physically and otherwise.

## 6.

### You'll Bloom When You're Goddamned Ready

woke up hungover and hungry at thirty-six with a strange man in my bed. It was the first time I'd slept with anyone on a first date. That's not because of a rule or moral stance, I'd just never met a person and felt that I *needed* to jump his bones immediately. For me, the best part of the date was the after, when, if it was good, I could go home, order food, watch TV, and daydream about the guy. If it was bad, I got to do all of that minus the daydreaming, which didn't even matter because of the sheer joy I experienced being back home, no longer on a shitty date. Sex with people I didn't know just wasn't that interesting. Yes, leaving the preordained space where a man and I had agreed to meet for a roughly preordained time would mean I no longer had control of my angles and edges, but the truth is that I only like spending a lot of time with people I really, really like, and I don't really, really like most people the first time I meet them. The energy drain of first-date sex always seemed like it would negate any potential thrill.

But then, suddenly, right there next to me, the morning after our very first, very mediocre date, was a man named Jason. Something made me take him home. He'd asked to, but lots of first dates had asked to and I'd never said yes before. I remembered only snippets of our night together. I knew he went to a Very Impressive College that he mentioned numerous times, even though we were almost forty. I knew there were moments we clashed, like when he called me a princess and I gave him hell for it, but bickering is often how I communicate with people I end up liking. I knew he'd said something about losing a lot of weight recently and I felt comforted by the idea of dating someone who probably understood my food anxiety.

I didn't recall the sex itself, and now it was the morning, and he was still here. More notably, I was not dying for him to leave.

Finally, he spoke: "I want to turn over, but I don't want you to see my scars."

"What do you mean?" I asked.

"I was in a fire, two years ago," he said. He said he thought it was his fault.

The details dripped out—he said he'd been drinking, sleepy, there was a lit cigarette, the apartment burned. In my bed, he turned onto his stomach, and I saw what he was talking about.

"Holy fuck," I said. "This is crazy."

I didn't mean that the story was crazy, though if I had been listening more closely I would have realized it was, in a way that should have alarmed me. I meant it was crazy that a man was in my bed, telling me he was worried about my seeing his body. And not just his body, his *back*. I told him that. I told him everything.

Eventually he needed to go, and by then I wanted him to, mostly so I could be alone with my imagination to process this amazing man I'd met. He was smart and funny; he was damaged in ways I could relate to, and he seemed to like me.

He sat on the edge of my bed as he got ready to leave. "Thank you for putting up with my foibles," he said, "and my wiener." I giggled. Nobody had thanked me for sleeping with them before. I thought he was adorable.

I was still smiling when I heard the front door click shut. I didn't replay all the lovely moments of our date because there weren't any. I didn't daydream about the feeling of his body on top of mine because the sex was a drunken blur. I didn't even really stop to think about whether or not I liked him because I already practically loved him. *This is it,* I thought. *This is the guy. I've finally found him.*

I emailed and texted Jason constantly. I decided I was too old to play games and was just going to let him know that I liked him. My usual aversion to vulnerability was gone because it felt like we had an understanding: There was something about our pairing that seemed predestined, and I wanted to make it absolutely clear I was in so he felt comfortable. I didn't know yet that "comfortable" wasn't a thing he ever felt.

For our second date, he came to trivia night with my friends, and I beamed with pride as he got literally every answer right. I didn't even really mind when he grabbed the pen out of my hand and assigned himself the job of recording our team's answers, often without consulting any of us. I smiled at my friends—*I brought a ringer, isn't he great?*—and though the night wasn't as much fun as usual, we took home first place.

For our third date, I picked a neighborhood bistro where I'd always wanted to go with someone special. It's warm and Brooklyn-y, and I'd only ever been there with friends or family. Now I got to go with a man I saw a potential future with, and I was elated. I got to look like all the couples I'd always envied there. Another box about to be checked.

When Jason arrived, he was formal and odd. It felt like we were starting from the beginning. I was disappointed. I told him so.

"I get so excited to see you," I said, "and then you're always so weird." He dropped his head in his hands. What I'd said wasn't nice, but I was just so confused. We'd slept together already. We knew each other's stories. I didn't get why we weren't moving forward at the pace I'd decided we should. So we finished our frisée salads and steak frites and lots and lots of wine and went to a bar around the corner. We drank more. We analyzed the date while we were on it. There was a tension there—one we both liked—and a drama building that we fed off of, but we didn't get along, exactly.

"You seem like an angry person," I said.

"How could you know that?" he asked. "I haven't told you that yet."

I shrugged, said that angry people don't have to tell anybody they're angry, it's usually pretty obvious.

Outside we smoked cigarettes, which I hadn't done in a long time but he did a lot.

"I don't know what's going on here," I said.

"I want to say something but I shouldn't," he replied.

"Say it. I think I know what it is."

"I wanted to say that I love you."

"I knew that was it. I love you, too."

We didn't have a lot of fun together or connect in the way I'm used to connecting with people, but there was something there, and now we'd put a name to it. There was some deep, indescribable connection, and now he'd said he felt it, too.

The morning after he told me he loved me, he told me again: "I thought I should say it sober."

It was official. We were in love. He was the first man I'd ever said it to. We'd known each other a month.

I once interviewed an Academy Award winner who told me that she's naturally very shy. She's so shy, she said, she gets embarrassed when people sing "Happy Birthday" to her.

All evidence points to the contrary. Her performances, her talk-show appearances, her social media—it all paints a picture of an effortless woman who is not only not shy but is an active spotlight seeker, someone who converts attention to fuel and might cease to exist were it not for the energy-giving gaze of others. She seems to thrive, not wilt, in the spotlight.

Maybe she is as shy as she says and just so good at acting (because she is incredibly good at acting) that she doesn't seem it. Or maybe she was once shy and no longer is but still relates to that little girl who couldn't stomach the fourteen seconds it took people to sing in her honor once a year. Maybe she thinks shy is somehow more venerable than not shy and is uncomfortable admitting that she has become a narcissistic creature of need when it comes to the attention of others, so she tells herself and others that she is shy, at her core, even if she's really not anymore.

My point is that sometimes from inside a life it's hard to tell what's true and what was once true; what felt like it would always be but isn't anymore and hasn't been for a long time.

I spent most of my life being boy crazy. Guys and dating and love occupied acreage in my brain, outdone, space-wise, only by my fear of rejection and humiliation. When I was little and played pretend with friends, I always wanted the scenarios to involve meeting up with guys and having sex. When I drew, I nearly always depicted scenes of couples holding hands and kissing. I was a little horndog. But.

My adolescent years, going all the way back to middle school, were most succinctly and accurately represented by a state of pining. I was a perpetual piner—nothing ever came to fruition, but I'd also never really thought through what fruition would look like. I was in many ways an innocent. When there were hints—a guy in high school idled in the driveway when he dropped me home after a night out, a twenty-two-year-old counselor at Pitch Pine Woods who often told me I was pretty stood very close one night—I physically bolted, my body making the swift decisions my ambivalent brain could not. I be-grudgingly, half-heartedly resolved to being a forever piner, though an optimistic one, because no matter how hard I tried to crush my own spirit, I was never completely successful.

I didn't have my first kiss until I was nineteen—drunk, Daisy Buchanan's bar in Boston, some guy whose name I don't re-member or never knew—and I did it because I was panicked about how quickly I was falling behind. It had nothing, not one smidge of a particle resembling a thing, to do with feelings in my body and what I wanted to do with them. As Nameless Guy poked around my mouth with his tongue, he grabbed my ass and I squirmed away; in the real world, the one that lived out-side my imagination, I hadn't thought about anything that might happen after the kiss.

That same year, word got out that some of the guys on my floor had rated the girls. When it was my turn, so the story went, Billy, my neighbor, had refused to rate me because it seemed unfair. I don't know what words he used exactly—because of her "condition" or "disease" or "deformity"—but it was clear what he meant. For better or worse (for better *and* worse, because I both desperately wanted and did not want to be rated), I couldn't be included with all the other girls because the playing field was not level. It would be unkind to include me, Billy thought. I had to be left out, but it wasn't my fault.

There it was again: I was an asterisk. Always.

The closest I came to having sex in college (which, to be clear, was *not at all close*) was junior year, when Bivan, one of the members of the all-boys a cappella group, took a shine to me. This sort of thing had happened before—good-looking charmers saw something in me that others didn't. It acted as confirmation that my face was truly as astonishing as my mother and other people had always told me it was, that they saw the real me (as opposed to the fake me, which was my body). Their seeing me was proof that they were some sort of soul mate. That's all it took, the seeing. Bivan did, and I was elated.

As a member of the Dear Abbeys, he was a very popular fixture with a certain set of nerdy girls; a big man maybe not on campus at large, but of a geeky horned-up corner of it. He showed up at my dorm and left notes on my bed when I wasn't home. He had a convertible—ridiculous for a school with Boston winters—and we drove around aimlessly. He started calling me whenever he felt like it, often at two A.M., and I'd groggily drag the phone into the hallway so I didn't wake my roommate, Lauren.

One night he asked what I was wearing.

"Um, a T-shirt and sweats?" I said.

He asked if I preferred one-piece or two-piece bathing suits at the beach.

"One-piece, always."

He asked if there were things I wouldn't do. Before I could ask for clarification—what do you mean *do*? Do *when*?—he said, "I draw the line at blood sports."

To me our conversation seemed like a battery of non sequiturs, as if he were on the other end filling out a *Mademoiselle* quiz, but when I told Lauren about it the next day, she informed me that Bivan was trying to have phone sex.

"Did his breathing change?" she asked, and I said I wasn't sure. The idea seemed inconceivable because he hadn't even tried to kiss me yet.

Eventually, Bivan stopped calling.

This is how things went for a very long time. I was convinced, in that dramatic way adolescents get convinced of such things, that I would die a virgin.* I'd sometimes become friends with guys I quietly fell in love with. I would listen for hours as they talked about the girls they liked. I'd help them make their move if the object of their affection was a friend of mine while silently screaming inside, "Pick me. Please god, pick me. Why won't anybody pick me?"

It was all the same. The dieting, the men: There was no end result I was working toward, which is a nice idea for an inspirational poster—"Forget the destination, enjoy the journey!"— but an exhausting proposition if it's how you're actually living your life. Or, it could be a wonderful way to live your life if you weren't, somewhere deep, terrified about never hitting the destination, which, again, you can't even name, but where it seems everyone else around you has already arrived.

I was not a Puritan—I have been a liberal, always—but I was also not a libertine. The world of men and sex and experience just didn't apply to me in the real world, I thought, even though I spent so much of my life fixated on all of it. It simply

---

* "Virgin" is yet another word I no longer use. You do not "lose" anything when you decide to have sex—especially not your virtue or your value— which means the idea of "losing one's virginity" is man-made, oppressive, and really fucking stupid.

existed in a different realm from the one in which I dwelled, and I worried that it might always be like that. I didn't like it—I *desperately* wanted romance and male attention, and I was never not in agony over someone—but I saw no way out.

There was no way out because I didn't realize the things I was doing. I didn't know that I was guarded. I didn't realize I could be cold and that my sarcasm was less like teasing and more like an electrified fence. I knew I was aloof but thought that was the same as being sexy and mysterious. I had not unlearned the preschool way of flirting—be mean, be indifferent, be removed—and had no clue that I'd built a barrier around myself, which was, when you got right down to it, what I wanted.

Even though I eventually recognized that I was the barrier builder, until very recently, I still had regrets that were pointless to have. *I could have been having sex in college,* I'd think. I could have been spending the night in boys' dorm rooms and sneaking off into secluded library stacks to get some. I didn't want any, not really, but I would conveniently ignore that when I was busy torturing myself. *I could have been having so much fun, if only I'd been ready!*

I wasn't ready, and I had plenty of fun. I loved college. But my lack of action would later haunt me because of what I thought it signified: lost chances, acting out of fear. I was acting out of instinct, but it took me a long time to see it that way. When I finally did have sex, it was because I decided to, with someone I didn't know very well: Theo, my best friend Amy's intern, who pursued me and then turned into my first boyfriend without my trying. I was twenty-four, ticking another box on the invisible scorecard in my head.

After Theo, I went right into a relationship with a grad school friend, Henry. After Henry, I spent all of my late twenties and most of my thirties either out with men or talking to men about going out. I had never really set my mind to dating; I figured I might as well try. (If you're thinking, *That sentence sounds familiar, didn't she say the same thing about dieting?* gold star for you!)

Once, in a Bushwick dive, the bartender placed my drink on a coaster and said, "I think we've been talking on OkCupid." Another day, as I walked past a sidewalk café in the East Village, a man having a meal there squinted at me and said, "Carla?" He was someone I had plans with the following week. I could give long walking tours of most New York City boroughs based on the places I've had dates; I could round a street corner at any moment and come upon someone I've kissed. My friend Todd once had the idea of setting me up with a coworker, but when he sent a photo I realized we'd already been out. The trivia master at a local bar told my friend Meagan he thought I was pretty, and when she put us in touch, I realized we'd been out, too.

I went out with men I had no interest in just because they were persistent. I went out with men I was wildly attracted to who kept me at arm's length, seeing me monthly or less. I once went out with a guy who told me there was no way to know whether the accusations against Bill Cosby were true or if he'd been set up by Jews in the media (check, please!). Another who picked a burrito joint with no bathroom for our first meeting, then chastised me for not finishing my meal. Once, at the end of a forgettable date, the guy asked for my phone number, and when he plugged it in realized he already had it and we'd been out before (neither one of us remembered, that's how forgettable the first date also was). I went on a series of dates with a man who wanted only to walk, and though not liking to walk is an affront to most New Yorkers, I would rather be sitting. I went out with a Broadway actor I was madly attracted to who ghosted me, then went out with him again a decade later when we re-matched on a different app (I remembered him, he did not remember me). I went on first dates that made my knees wobble with excited anticipation, and others that scared me, not in a good way. I went out with the patient of a friend's therapist mom and found out what he thought of me based on things he said in his next session. I went on dates with finance bros who made more money than I knew a person could make. I went on a date with a man who was a busker in the subway. I went out with everyone, all the time. All they had to do was ask.

Occasionally I'd form a close and essentially platonic bond with a particular type of man, someone who was unavailable to me in some way (he could be married or just so self-absorbed that he wasn't really available to anyone), except the friendships always veered into the sexual in some way, with my knowing the sorts of details purely platonic friends usually don't. I ended up as what I've come to think of as a shock absorber, who received (nay, welcomed!) the tribulations of men because it gave me the illusion of being wanted in some way but the security of knowing nothing would ever come from it. I was some-one men felt comfortable sharing intimate details with because I am a good listener and not judgmental and I know how to balance levity with caring, and maybe they thought I was just a little bit pretty, so they could unload all their emotional tur-moil (and maybe an occasional dick pic), so it was fun, not like work or therapy, and because I took it, it gave me the illusion of closeness. (I do not recommend becoming a shock absorber, by the way. Any gratification it brings will eventually be out-weighed by a feeling of being left out in the cold, and not only that, but left out in the cold after functioning as a person-shaped emotional cum rag, so cold *and* damp.)

Dates and dalliances during my Era of Being Out There rico-cheted off me; though I didn't know it at the time, they were token experiences I was having just to say I had. I didn't stop to wonder what I was doing until I got old enough to find dating so exhausting that I couldn't see doing it anymore. Most of the men I fell for were the ones who told me tacitly, from the be-ginning, again and again, that I could never have them.

Tendency to disappear was the only common denominator in the men I was attracted to. If I had a type, it was elusive, meaning slippery, cannot-be-had men. I was attracted to eels. The guys I really liked—who were remote and for whom I was always performing, angling my body and pretending to care deeply about whatever it was they were passionate about, whether that was reggae or Ashtanga or foreign film—always disappeared. The men who were forthright about wanting to date me did not interest me in the slightest. The kind ones, the gentle ones, the ones who didn't play games or fuck with my head . . . *yawn.*

When I wasn't counting WeightWatchers Points at night, I was obsessively replaying the last email, text, or phone call I'd had with whatever man I was presently obsessing over, his every syllable clanging around my brain like a pinball, looking for signs and prognostications that he was slipping away from me.

Confusingly, at the opposite end of my inferiority complex was a superiority one. The confluence of my sexual awakening, first-time weight loss, and sheer desire to no longer miss out on the vaguely slutty life of a young New Yorker resulted in a sort of delusional overconfidence. During the time when I was dating incessantly, I felt personally offended and shocked anytime a man didn't flirt with me, even if he was married or maybe even gay; same goes for lesbians, even if they knew I was straight. I was flummoxed and angry if someone didn't seem entranced by me. *Haven't you heard, everybody? I'm all the rage now.* I picture my self-worth then like a trifle suddenly flipped on its head; all the same layers there, just inverted and no more stable. I had a few short-lived affairs to show for my years on the market, usually relationships that lasted a month or two. I got back together with Henry. We split again. I sort of gave up.

I went out with hundreds of men. I thought I was trying to make them all my husband or my boyfriend or my *something,* but I think my biggest goal was proving to myself, *You are a person, you are a woman, you deserve to be rated.*

I never asked the men I was out with whether they knew the truth about my body, if they had the full picture. Some said cryptic things that maybe weren't so cryptic—I got a text after a date once, the guy telling me, "I'm so sorry, I feel like I said something insensitive tonight," but I didn't know what he was talking about and wasn't interested enough in him to probe further. When Theo and I broke up, he said reassuringly, "I need you to know that this isn't about your body," which wasn't reassuring at all, because I hadn't thought it was about my body until he told me it wasn't.

Sometimes I'd wonder how dating would go if I didn't have my face. Or if my body *and* face were average but I were missing a finger. What about an entire arm? Both arms? How much of a person can you remove while leaving the personhood intact? I say almost all of it, save the heart and a lung and the brain, maybe less, but I've got skin in the game, which is a lose-lose one, by the way. There is no way to win it, at least not when you're playing the way I did. I feared these were the rules—the stupid, bigoted, horrible, shallow, ableist rules—men lived by, and I was perpetually afraid of being found out for breaking them.

Did I, you might be wondering, at any time stop to think about whether *I* liked these men whose appraisal I was becoming so increasingly dependent on? Yes! I disliked many of them, either because they bored me or weren't funny or were pompous or just weren't for me in the way people just aren't for each other sometimes. And yet, I gave them all the power. I thought they deserved it because they did not have a giant mass on their back and had matching legs. At least that's my assumption. I never asked. As you've probably gathered, all this thinking means I am sometimes self-involved.

There's that sobriety mantra—your secrets keep you sick—and I went through a few brief periods of overcorrection, blurting out that my body was fucked up on date one or two, and that went about as well as you'd imagine. It's not even that everybody rejected me, it's just that I was subjecting myself to a sort of forced exposure therapy that left me feeling like a wet, shaking animal. Mazel to me, I was able to talk about my body, but at what cost? My story should have been a gift doled out only to the most worthy. I should have seen it that way. I should have realized that anyone who had the privilege of hearing about it should have earned it through trust and care. Instead, once I worked up the courage, I started sputtering out information to anyone I was hoping would become my boyfriend—here, look at this, tell me what you think—which wasn't fair to me or to them. It was pure insanity. It was degrading—who cares how they rated me? I should have been focused on how I rated them—but it's where I had landed. It's exactly where I was when I met Jason.

After we said that we were in love, I kept waiting for Jason to break up with me, because I was used to that happening with men I really liked. One night I was sure he was going to end things. We were at a party and there was pot—lately I smoked whenever he did, which was a lot—and I was feeling edgy and picking fights.

"You keep leaving me alone," I said accusingly.

"I'm just talking to my friends," he said.

My sense of insecurity in the beginning stages of dating anyone was intense—everything felt built on quicksand. I was Little Miss Anxious Attachment, and the weed made it worse. When we left the party, I braced myself for the speech, one in which he said he'd made a mistake and it was over. Instead he smiled and squeezed my hand: "Let's go get a drink somewhere else," then, "I love you."

I felt pure relief. The "I love yous" came—from both of us—steadily now. We kept ourselves full on alcohol and I love yous. They meant "I'm sorry" and "It's okay" and "Don't worry" and occasionally "I love you." We were reassuring each other, because we sensed that we might not last, and we wanted to. That's an odd thing to think if you're really, genuinely happy, so we either must not have been or we'd both been so disappointed before that we felt like constant guarding and reassuring would guarantee our success. We both wanted this so much.

We didn't have a lot in common. He liked to spend time with his best friend, Bea, a frowny blah of a woman he'd once dated, playing video games in dive bars—*actual* dive bars, the kind old alcoholics go to, not the hipster imitations I preferred—and biking around the city. I liked getting dressed up and going to brunch for seven hours with groups of people. Even the things we both enjoyed, like the beach, we enjoyed in different ways: He preferred Fort Tilden, which was accessible only by bike or on foot and was populated by Brooklyn stoners and women sunbathing topless; I liked Jacob Riis, which had clean bathrooms and concessions and parking you could pay for.

We spent weeknights watching TV and ordering in, and once Saturday came, we would splinter onto separate paths. He'd grab his bike—"Have a good day, babe!"—and do his thing while I did mine. We never had brunch. We tried, one Sunday—it felt like a failure to have a boyfriend and not participate in that sacred Brooklyn ritual—but when we got to the bus stop, the M65 was pulling away, so we went to a coffee shop down the street that we'd been to before and ordered stale bagels, eating them in silence as I pouted.

Pouting became my defining characteristic. I pouted when we went out with his friends and he ignored me. I pouted when he'd get unexpectedly formal, saying, "Take care" as he left my apartment in the morning in a way that made me think I was never going to see him again. I pouted at my birthday party when I heard him talking to someone about a woman with "great tits." I pouted (and consoled him) at a bar when he and a buddy had a disagreement and, Jason told me a few minutes later, he'd punched a hole in the wall. I pouted anytime I felt he was not living up to what I had decided he should be, in any and all ways.

I'm sure all my pouting was exhausting.

Sometimes I left the bar and decided I wasn't talking to him. I almost always told him what he had done to disappoint me, which I guess wasn't very nice. Annie said she'd never seen me cry so much, and she's known me since high school.

It's just that we had so much potential and he was botching it—he was so awkward; how could a person be *so* awkward?—dropping his face into his hands again and again, the most natural position I'd see him in over the course of our relationship. I was asking him, again and again, without realizing it, to be a different person. If he could just be a different person, maybe this could work.

Each of us was on a doctor-prescribed cocktail of psychotropic meds, and Jason decided to stop his mood stabilizer cold turkey. I asked why, and he shrugged. He said he would stay on his antidepressant. He'd definitely stay on the alcohol and grass. We didn't talk about it any more than that. He was warning me again, I'd think later, he was giving me a way out. But I was in love. It was enough. It was all I'd ever wanted.

When his lease was up, six months into our relationship, he gave Bea his cat and moved into my apartment.

All those years of dating before Jason were not about securing a partner in life—they were about proving to myself that I was a person who did things that people do. I went out. I slept with guys. I'd be devastated when men would ghost me, sad when I'd demand commitment from someone not ready to give it. Those feelings were real. But after years of going out on as many as four dates a week, I'm not sure I ever actually wanted a boyfriend. I certainly wanted men to adore me, but did I want someone in my space and my life all the time? I don't know.

There was a short stretch of time in my single thirties, pre-Jason, when I wasn't dating much. Every Saturday I would wake up and feel nothing but promise: of a day spent meandering the city alone, or with friends in bars and stores and restaurants, of all the things a Saturday brings after a long week. But on Sunday, just as surely, I would wake in a state of terror with the feeling that I would be doing this—waking up alone, in this apartment, in this bed—for the rest of my life. I never stopped to wonder if that was such a bad thing; I focused only on the gut reaction. It was like that for a very long time. Exhilaration followed by doom. It meant, I didn't know yet, that I would end up with the first person willing to slide comfortably into my life, regardless of whether he was the right person, the wrong person, or the worst person.

The night Jason met my parents, they were running late.

"Where *are* they?" he asked, and I said I didn't know. I was used to this—we are a running-late family—and what was the big deal? I figured they'd get there when they got there. Jason seemed to me like a toddler on the verge of a tantrum.

The restaurant was crowded and loud, and my mother made us move tables once, which is less than her average. The move put us extremely close to a table populated by a loud, drunken foursome. The din in the place was a neurodivergent's nightmare, which meant it was probably plucking the nerves of three of the four of us at the table (congrats on being neurotypical, Dad!).

My mother immediately liked Jason. He was so quick, so intellectual, he went to that Very Impressive College, he got every reference my parents made, which was not nothing. Conversations with my mom and dad can feel like an intellectual gauntlet, and if you don't keep up, you might walk away with the distinct feeling that you have failed in some way, because you have. But not Jason. My mother kicked me under the table and mouthed, "I like him."

The table next to us seemed to be getting louder. And I didn't realize that every time a waiter or busboy walked by, they knocked into Jason's chair. I did not know that the combination of every bump with every obnoxious utterance was notching up the temperature of his mood. I did not know he was a pot about to boil over. I can't remember who said what first. One of the guys had insulted him somehow. Maybe he invaded his space. It all happened very quickly.

Suddenly, Jason and one of the guys from the other table were standing up, face-to-face, very close. Somehow I was standing between them. I was confused about everything except for the fact that they were absolutely about to fight.

I held Jason's face and repeated his name over and over— "Jason, Jason, stop, Jason"—but he didn't hear me. I could not reach him. I was having a conversation with a wall.

My parents said his name, too, but he would not sit down. Neither would the other guy.

I burst into tears and fled to the front of the restaurant, where a waitress put her arm around me. Waiters somehow got the other guy and his friends out the door. The waitress somehow got me back to the table. It was all relatively short and fast.

They were just being so rude, Jason said once we were all seated again, and the waiters and waitresses agreed—that table was a nightmare, they appreciated Jason's standing up for them—and they brought us complimentary champagne as gratitude. He was, somehow, a hero.

I sobbed through the rest of dinner, which somehow continued.

Somehow, somehow, somehow.

Outside, afterward, my parents kissed us goodbye and my mother told Jason, "It was so good to meet you!" and "See you at Thanksgiving!"

Once Jason and I got upstairs, he admonished me: "You didn't look at me once. After the fight, you didn't look at me once."

I had abandoned him. I let him down. He was disappointed in me. He felt betrayed.


My friends and his friends all asked how dinner was.

"It was great!" I said, then told them about the fight.

One by one they kind of scrunched up their noses and said some version of "But it was *great*?"

"Oh," I said, "yeah. Other than that it went really well."

I was not putting on a brave face; I thought I was telling the truth.

"My parents really loved him!" I said, and I meant it or thought I did. They didn't check in after dinner to see if I was okay, which must have meant they didn't think they needed to, which must have meant that I was okay. It's true, my parents tend to mind their own business and avoid stepping on my toes if they're afraid it will upset me, but I believed my mom when she said she liked him. It all added up to dinner being great.

I did not realize that I sounded absolutely insane.

Jason and I talked, vaguely, about getting married.

I worried about the fact that I spent so many mornings hung-over.

He told me I was beautiful.

He accidentally called me Bea more and more.

His chaos excited me.

Sometimes when he was sleepy, in the morning, he'd call me Mom.

I was a regular person with regular boyfriend issues!

I was sometimes a little afraid of him.

It was getting harder and harder to tell if I was happy because I couldn't remember what happiness was supposed to feel like.

After a string of incels made the news for incidents of varying degrees of violence against women, Jason said he wanted to write an essay about relating to them, to tell the story of how in an alternate universe, he could have ended up a homicidal maniac, too. In his draft, which I read, he confessed to misogyny and misanthropy and emotional abuse when he was younger; and the fact that he'd gotten fired from a job because after watching his office crush leave a work party with another man, he'd shouted, "My life would be better if that bitch were dead."

His point was that he once related to these monsters but had come out the other side and wanted to let other angry young men know that they could too.

The only concrete piece of feedback I offered was for him to

make sure he wanted this out there, because, I knew from experience, once it was on the internet, there was no going back.
Otherwise, I told him I thought the piece was good, because it
was. And I understood what he was doing: He wanted to be
published. He was using his ugly past to do it, just as I'd used my
body.

A national website bought and posted the essay.

A couple of friends told me they found it alarming.

Jason lost his job again. He was fuzzy on the details, and I
asked few questions. I got the sense that his coworkers were no
longer comfortable with him around.

He was already living with me. Now he was living with me
and had nowhere to go during the day.

The worst night we had together was in 2015, when I was
working long hours as a deputy editor. I had stopped getting my
period, which I knew was due to stress, not pregnancy, because
we rarely had sex.

I'd also developed an abscess on my inner thigh, which was
getting worse by the day; its placement meant repeated friction
when I walked, for I am not a thigh-gap girl. It was the size of a
tea saucer by the time I saw a doctor. She prescribed Vicodin,
which I'd taken the night Jason burst into the apartment with
a problem.

"Babe, we have an issue," he shouted from the doorway, and
I heard his bike clang against the wall. I'd asked him repeatedly
to stow it in the basement bike room, but he wouldn't. I shuffled out, high on opioids, legs cowboy-wide so I wouldn't irri-

tate the fissure. His arm was gushing. He'd fallen off his bike, he said. He thought we needed to go to the hospital.

We hailed a cab instead of calling an ambulance because we thought it would be faster; both of us tried to stay calm as we put pressure on the blood-soaked towel we'd tied tight around his arm. The taxi crawled in the direction of the hospital, and when the driver rolled up to a red light on a sleepy brownstone street and stopped, Jason instructed him to go.

"There's nobody here, you can turn," he said.

"It's red," the driver replied.

"I'm in a lot of pain. I'm bleeding."

"Then you should have called an ambulance."

He was right, of course, but Jason was angry. He began to mimic the man in a nondescript stereotypical Indian accent, like Apu from *The Simpsons*: "Then you should have called an ambulance," he parroted back in a seething minstrelsy.

I was crying suddenly, a bit hysterically. "What are you doing?" I shouted at Jason. "Stop it!" I was horrified. We were *good people.*

He said the next part to me loudly and slowly. "Will you for once [beat] in your goddamned life [beat] shut your fucking mouth?" I'd chosen our cab driver's dignity over my boyfriend, and now I was going to pay for it. There was a sadistic snarl in his voice, a pitch I'd heard before but only directed at others. The first person I'd heard him talk to like this—using these exact words, actually—was a family member on the phone. I'd come home and he was pacing the apartment, in the midst of berating her, calling her a whore, telling her to kill herself. I don't know what set him off. He was shaken afterward and promised me, unbidden, "I will never do that to you. I will never, ever speak to you that way." He was trying to promise himself that it would never happen by saying it out loud, but I think we both knew it was a guarantee that someday of course it would.

Once we arrived at the hospital, he admonished me multiple times. As we waited for him to be admitted, he beckoned me outside and said—voice eerily calm, so much worse than the yelling—that I could not talk to him the way I did. *Did I understand?* he asked. *Did I understand that I could not talk to him the way I had talked to him tonight?*

Later, around two or three in the morning, after I'd spent hours waiting for him to be stitched up, trying to figure out what I would do—*Will I leave him? Will he let me?*—we waited outside for our Uber home. Something I did triggered him and he called me a "spoiled little Jewish girl." That finally undid me.

"Shut the fuck up!" I exploded, and now I'd crossed another milestone off the list I didn't know I was keeping: Get into a hysterical screaming match in the street with your boyfriend. I was just like other people. I was so lucky.

In the car he taunted me as I sobbed: "It's always about *you*," he said over and over until we got home. The only other thing he said was at the apartment door—"I'll grab my stuff and go to Bea's"—and when he left, I was relieved to be able to chain the door.

I woke up to long texts explaining that it had been the pain talking, his injury was excruciating, that wasn't really him, he was so sorry. My therapist, whom I called from work first thing in the morning, still crying, suggested that Jason stay away at least one more night, and when I asked him for that, he said no, it was his home, too. Those words petrified me; I realized I had never, even during our best times, thought of it as his home; I didn't want it to be his home.

When I got back from work that night, there were flowers on the coffee table and a hangdog look on his face. I could not believe this was happening to me. I couldn't believe I was a woman who got flowers from a boyfriend who yelled at her. I did not know how I'd gotten here.

Still, we tried to repair what we'd lost. A few days later, Jason and I sat in a bar getting drunk, and he said, "If we're going to make this work, you have to take responsibility for your part in it, too."

That was the moment I knew I was fucked, when things finally clicked and I worried I might be in a situation I could not get out of. I saw things stacked up and didn't know how I hadn't put all the pieces together before: His apartment had burned down. He told a relative to kill herself. He wrote an article in a national publication about the time in his life when he took pleasure in tormenting women. I was always crying and always drunk.

I suggested couples counseling, and he grudgingly agreed. We made it to one session. Afterward, the therapist told Marilyn, who told me, "Carla is a powerhouse, and Jason is scary." Both things shocked me and were also obvious. I could see why I might seem like a powerhouse, but I was a powerhouse whose battery was dying.

We got into another fight, I don't remember about what, and when he went downstairs to smoke a cigarette in the middle, I fled. He sent taunting texts once he realized I'd gone, accusing me of being a coward. I ran to Annie's apartment two blocks away, looking over my shoulder the whole time. The me that was now outside of me was wondering, *When did you become a person who has to run from not-her-apartment while looking over her shoulder?*

In the end, he was the one who pulled the plug. I don't know how much longer I would have stayed if he hadn't, but I hope not much. We were meeting for a drink after I'd gone to work, and he told me that Bea had a friend with a spare room he could move into.

"Like break up?" I asked. He said yes.

I declared that I wanted to leave the bar immediately, that I wanted him to pack up his stuff and text me when he was done, that I did not want to be there when it was happening. He could come back another day when I wasn't around and get the rest of it. For someone who spends so much time anticipating the worst, trying to ward off endings with magical thinking, I am decisive once those things happen. I do not like to dwell. Jason's presence in my apartment was my body after I gave up surgery: I wanted it erased and never spoken of again. I wanted him to leave no trace.

After he cleared out his stuff for good, he left a bulleted note that included things like "I love you" and "Never forget all the fun we had," and I tried to think of one time we'd had fun: not because we were drunk, not because someone else made us laugh, but one time when we'd had true, unadulterated fun together, *because* of each other.

I couldn't.

The thing is, and I mean this, I never, ever think about him. But I do have to look back and ask why, for thirteen months of my life—that's all it amounted to—I not only let this person in but made gigantic efforts to get him to stay.

I could make it a simple equation: I was so focused on being accepted that I hadn't bothered to look at anything else about the person doing the accepting. Or maybe, darker, I thought someone like Jason was the sort of person I deserved, even though I can happily tell you now that I really, *really* do not think that. I got the one thing I claimed to want—unconditional acceptance of my body—but forgot to check whether I wanted everything else that came with it.

But it's not that simple, because I'd already had versions of that. These men aren't the point. They never were. Did I really want somebody who would reject me for my looks? Hardly. Would I stand for it if that sort of rejection happened to a friend? No, I'd probably demand the person's number and hatch an elaborate, potentially criminal plan for revenge. Maybe Jason and I have that in common.

I made my body the center of my issues because even though that felt hard, it was easy. It was my most useful and trusted scapegoat. I didn't end up with Jason because he was a man who accepted my deformity. I ended up with Jason because angry, brilliant men were once my safe space, and because as much as I claimed to hate chaos, it was where I felt most alive.

What I for so long wrote off as a lack of experience due to circumstance was, I think, self-determination. Where it came from is another story (years of self-protection, of flinching too soon to avoid something terrible), but it was all my choice. All those years I thought of myself as a victim of circumstance, I was making decisions. Age made me realize the difference, simple as that.

Now I don't regret all the experiences I didn't have. I regret only that I wasted so much time regretting them instead of just appreciating all the fun I *was* having. There would be time for men. So much time. Too much time.

I don't feel like any more or less of a person because of all my experience. Again, twenty-year-old me would not believe it, but it's true. As is so often the case, the thing I was looking for was never the thing.

Like that shy actor when people sing "Happy Birthday," I sometimes still tell myself stories. When I think about my life, I think of myself as an innocent, even though I am unequivocally not one anymore. I don't know why I do this, what comfort it brings, because it must bring some, even if it's cold. I have this idea that there is some real me out there, stuck in the '90s, before my brain had even finished developing, that is a truer version of me than the one that is sitting here typing. The Platonic ideal of me-ness? It's not real, but also maybe it doesn't matter? Maybe the same way I see the futility and harm of labels like "late bloomer" and "virgin," there's no actual benefit to my figuring out where I fall, whether I have been slutty enough to consider myself experienced or experienced enough to consider myself a person. I am one. Whether or not I believe it can't change that.

I have no idea how my romantic story ends. (Sorry, first agent who said it would be easier to sell my book if I had a boyfriend. Also, hey, look: I sold my book without having a boyfriend!) Aging, the pandemic . . . it's all made the idea of dating sound even more exhausting. I am out of practice. There have been men since Jason, but mostly I've been single. Do I envision marriage for myself? Probably not, because I don't see the point and the idea of tethering myself to someone legally and financially stresses me out. What about a committed relationship? Sure, I guess. If it were the right person. If it's a person who improves the quality of my life. If it's a person I trust and who makes me feel cared for and safe and calm and happier than I am when I'm alone. If that person exists for me.

There was a time when admitting that on paper would have terrified me—what is the point of life if you do not have someone to love who loves you back?—but now it really doesn't, because I have a lot of people I love who love me back. The Carla who flitted around the city in her twenties and thirties trying to impress men would absolutely not believe there would come a time when she truly would not care whether she ever found a person. But finding a person is only a prize if it's a good person, who you enjoy spending time with, who you can be yourself around. Someone you are not afraid of, who is not an eel. Being happily single is not a last resort, it is fucking rad. If you don't believe me, that's okay. What matters is that I do.

# 7.

## *Your Body Is Not a Temple, It's a Party Hall*

have spent so much time fixated on diets and men. I wish I
hadn't. But I have spent just as much time fixated on fashion,
and for that I am grateful, despite the pitfalls.

Accurately explaining what it feels like to be a compulsive
shopper means picking any random day as an example, because
they're all more or less the same. Here's a recent one: I saw a
metallic silver jacquard ruffled minidress on the Ganni site. It
was exquisite, and just under five hundred dollars, which did
not seem outrageous. I usually find jacquard stuffy (everyone
has a favorite-fabric hierarchy, right?), but something about the
silver made it amazing. The dress went up only to a Danish 44,
the equivalent of a US 14, the size I most identify with but
haven't actually been in years. This is because when I was
growing up, I had to reach for whatever the biggest size was,
and the absolute biggest you could hope for was a 14, ergo, I was

a 14, even when a 14 didn't fit. I have been shopping long enough to know that sizing is often haphazard and unreliable, so you don't know until you know. I had one main worry about the dress: Just under the bust, at what looked like the exact place on my body where an errant curve of flesh bulges out, was an unforgiving-looking seam. But I had to try.

*You never know.*

When the dress arrived, I was still excited about it, which is rare. The exhilaration usually starts to wane at the moment of purchase; often by the time the thing arrives I am already over it. But I was even *more* excited about the Ganni dress in person—the silver was practically robotic looking. It would be a conversation starter.

So much of my wardrobe starts conversations, and I love being at the center of them. I have been to parties where people tell me I have the best outfit of the night, even when there are many showstoppers in the room. It's something I usually already know but love to hear anyway.

Only, I couldn't get the Ganni dress on. The seam I had expected to thwart me did, and it was impossible to budge the material any farther than my collarbone. *Return it,* my inner voice said, but it was drowned out by another one: *Don't give up yet.*

I googled and found an Upper East Side tailor who had worked with every important designer around, including ones I love and wear (Acne Studios, Christian Siriano). I emailed and explained my predicament. The tailor encouraged me to come in and see what he could do.

Before our appointment, an idea took hold: "What if I buy a

second dress? Will that make alterations potentially easier?" Yes, the tailor said, that was a good idea. Many of his clients— who I imagined to be ladies who lunch married to men who bank—did this sort of thing. I was basically supplying him with extra fabric, and I was happy to do it.

The second dress arrived, in a 42 because the 44 was now sold out—I suspect I was the owner of their lone "big" size—so I had now spent around a thousand dollars when you included tax and shipping on two dresses in two different sizes that did not fit. My bank account was overdrawn. My credit cards were both perilously close to being maxed out. But I couldn't *not* have the dress.

I went for my initial fitting (a not-fitting, since more of the dress was off my body than on). The tailor was excited—this was going to be such a fun project!—and I mentioned that maybe I would wear the dress to my book party, something I knew was a lie because my book party was at least two years away and by then I would have found many other things that I had decided were my book-party dress and I would have already worn this metallic masterpiece—to dinner, to a play, in my apartment for one selfie, wherever—because I would not have been able to wait.

Because I am not a dressmaker, alterations often seem simple to me when they're not. Just sew them together! What could be hard about that? I was ecstatic.

Days went by, then a call from the tailor's assistant: They had an estimate for the alteration. The words came out slowly and what I thought was going to be "two hundred dollars" ended up sounding like "two thousand dollars," so I asked the tailor's assistant to please repeat that: "Two thousand dollars," she said, and that's the moment my brain reentered my skull. I asked when I could come pick up the dresses because no, I could not spend two thousand dollars.

What followed was an inner debate of whether to try to find another tailor or contact Ganni to see if I was too late to start a return, and if not, whether they would send me new mailing labels; I'd discarded mine when the dresses arrived because I could not foresee a reality in which we would willingly part.

In defeat, I chose the latter. I explained the situation. Ganni said it was fine. They sent my return labels. I put the dresses in the mail. It was over.

Is that the dumbest thing you've ever read? It's embarrassing. But that's compulsive shopping. I needed that dress; I didn't stop needing it, I was just kneecapped because there was no real way I could see paying three thousand dollars for something that was supposed to be five hundred. I didn't know where the money would come from; I was already unsure about how I was going to pay down my credit card bills *before* the prospect of another three thousand dollars.

Sometimes that's when the worst of it happens. When I'm already deep in it, sometimes I lean in and think, *It's already bad, why not make it worse? I could be dead tomorrow. The earth is melting. Everybody has an AR-15. People have no homes. Trans people are being hunted. Antisemitism is somehow cool again. Buy the dress.*

The only privilege as competitive as thinness and conventionality when it comes to fashion is means: If you have wealth, you can afford beautiful clothes, and if straight sizes don't fit and you have the money, you can afford to have your clothes custom-made, something most couturiers will do. It comes at a price—you owe them for the bespoke patternmaking—but if you have the cash, you'll be grateful for the opportunity to pay more than your thin, regular-bodied peers for the same exact product. I had the money, then didn't, but I kept shopping anyway because I could not stop.

My mother's mother, Grandma Rae, was prone to flights of fancy that would send my parents on escapades across the city to locate her in the middle of the night when I was young. She once confused day for night and was found patiently waiting at four A.M., in the dark, on the doorsteps of her doctor's office, which she'd taken three buses to get to. Another time she nearly blinded herself with medicated shampoo because she'd become convinced she had lice (she did not).

Clothing was very important to her. Her family was wealthy before they emigrated from Turkey, but she was poor by the time she married my Hungarian grandfather in New York, and she did what she could with what she had. When my mother and Aunt Margie were little, Grandma Rae would take them to Loehmann's and Alexander's, and if they found something they liked but not in the right size, Grandma might buy two, then ask her seamstress Susan to sew them together or buy one way too big and have Susan take it in. Even though she had next to nothing, Grandma Rae had Susan, and she had a second seamstress on standby in case Susan wasn't free. When Grandma Rae had to have something, she *had* to have it; she made it happen no matter how sparse her resources.

When I was a kid, in the winter, my mom would shove her cold hands into the back of my sweater every morning and command, "Walk away from me! Walk away from me!" She'd pull, pull, pull as I marched forward but stayed in place on an invisible treadmill designed to loosen the tight fibers that were not meant to be bodycon but were on me. Clothes were always there, like a bitchy friend I could depend on only some of the time, but who I always wanted to be close to.

As I got older I spent evenings in dresses that made it hard to breathe, just to show that I could. I taught two-hour writing classes standing in pairs of boots that made my right foot throb, then tingle, then go numb, because that felt like a better option than not wearing the boots. Finding a pair of pants that fit one leg but not the other was the ultimate slap in the face (looking at you, stretch leather leggings), and sometimes I would buy them anyway. I'd make stretching out the leather of the right leg a monthslong project.

Long before the internet, the credits pages of magazines helped me scratch the itch of consumption, and my mom assisted. I am so grateful for it. I inherited her passion, as she inherited hers from her mother, who inherited hers from her also manic-depressive mother. I grew up going to department stores where salespeople knew our names. It seemed as normal as Nose Job Gym.

I can still see the cover of *Seventeen* when I was eleven, a model jumping in the air wearing what looked like a gold crinoline tutu. I showed my mom and she was equally awestruck. The credits said it was Betsey Johnson, from Bloomingdale's, so my mother got to work, calling all the Bloomie's until she found it in stock. We were in luck: The Paramus store just over the New Jersey border had one in a large, so we asked them to put it aside with my name on it and we three—my mother, father, and I—got into the car and headed northwest. I had worries—what if someone got there first and took it, what if it was too small?—but we made it in time, and the skirt fit. Not only that, there was a matching gold-lace blouse that hadn't featured in *Seventeen,* and I got that, too. It felt like a glorious drug run.

I have friends in bigger bodies who grew up not allowed to wear anything their mothers deemed unflattering. My mom and I didn't always agree on what I should be wearing (in addition to having a congenital disorder, I also had mood swings and all the emotions that cause girls to sometimes fight with their mothers), but she has always agreed that clothing brings joy. Clothing is a celebration of the body, so by the transitive property (math!), my mother encouraged me to celebrate mine.

My fashion preferences and rules have fluctuated without any sense I can tease out other than the intrusion of hormones, trends, societal standards, boredom, and the unpredictable ebbs and flows of my self-confidence. Prepuberty, the only rules foisted upon me were by my mother, like no all-black outfits before fourth grade because black was too grown-up, and no two-piece bathing suits for reasons I was never told but knew. Anything else simply came down to whether I could get myself into it, and whether my mom liked it and thought it was worth whatever it cost.

In middle school, I wore shorts, including bike shorts when they came into fashion. In the early '90s, when Anna Wintour and Marc Jacobs ripped grunge from Kurt Cobain's hands and put it on covers and catwalks, I paired flimsy slip dresses with tartan flannels and Docs, but I would not wear the ribbed, clingy, 1960s-inspired poor-boy sweaters that came back into style around the same time. I liked those sweaters. I wanted one. Maybe if my hair were longer, if it went down to my waist like a curtain.

I wore a Betsey Johnson stretch-crushed-velvet dress to my sweet sixteen, even though it showed off the shape of my back at least as much as a poor-boy sweater would have. Maybe I wanted it more than I didn't want people to see my back.

Sometime around junior year, I bought my first bikini and wore it on group outings to the beach, even when boys were there, with an unbuttoned button-down over it.

In college I stopped wearing shorts but continued to wear stretchy fabrics, populating my wardrobe with Y2K mesh tops and dresses by Vivienne Tam and Jean-Paul Gaultier.

By the end of college and all of grad school, I would not let any skin other than my face, neck, shoulders, arms, and hands be seen. This meant all skirts shorter than Mennonite length went over jeans, the aforementioned sweater coats were a staple, a sweatshirt was perpetually tied around my waist, and I never wore sandals.

In my thirties, I began to explore shorter skirts, but only with tights and boots that came up very high, limiting the amount of leg exposed beneath the bottom of the skirt and the top of the boots. An inch of hosiery-clad leg; I could manage that. Most boots did not fit my right leg, so I had to forsake designer for synthetic plus-size brands that smelled of rubber, because when faced with the choice of not wearing the dress at all or wearing the dress with a pair of boots that degraded the outfit, the answer was clear.

After the *Marie Claire* article came out in 2009, I met other people with K-T for the first time, and one of them, a young woman named Ari, had photos of herself on social media in shorts and miniskirts and suddenly I remembered: I had done that once, too. I could do it again if I wanted to. Just seeing her was a reminder that I had made the decision to hide, and I could make the decision to unhide.

I started wearing shorts. I wore miniskirts with tights. I wore miniskirts *without* tights. I bought dresses so flimsy and small they were practically not there. By my late thirties I was wearing dresses so short, people thought they were shirts. I had many sheer tops that exposed my bra. Marilyn once expressed concern in session for my physical safety, she said, because my dress was so minuscule and see-through that she could see my underpants. I felt empowered—fuck anyone who doesn't like my back or my legs or my ass, that's their problem—but I think I was also testing them. Say something to me; stare at me. *I dare you.*

In the same way an outfit I loved could exalt me, one I didn't could destroy my mood. When Net-a-Porter and other sites started offering same-day delivery in New York, there were days I arrived to work in something I was not thrilled with and left in something entirely different. If I had a TV spot or a date or plans with friends or a man I wanted to impress, I might drop four hundred bucks on a new dress, plus twenty-five for hand delivery as if it were an emergency. Existing in an outfit that did not excite me, that did not announce me to the world in a way that represented who I was at that given moment, was as uncomfortable as that fucking back brace had been all those years ago. I could not tolerate it. I needed it off me immediately.

At forty-seven, I wear midriff-baring sets, two-piece bathing suits, leggings, dresses with cutout backs. The last one is the biggest shocker. My back is my OG deformity, even though I've had this whole body since birth. It was the real problem, the real difference, and I never imagined I would let anyone see it. And then suddenly, poof, I did, because I found a dress I couldn't *not* have: Mara Hoffman, billowy statement sleeves, lightweight cotton, perfect for summer gallivanting. The back dipped down farther than I was used to or comfortable with, but I bought it. Not only that, I made Melissa, a photographer, take a picture of me in it, a close-up of my back in the dress. It was an impulsive idea—most of my big ideas are impulsive and carried out before I have time to change my mind—and I posted that photo to Instagram. I wrote about how mind-blowing it was that I not only wanted to do it, but that I *did* it. The desire to have the dress, to put it on, to use it to show off, was more important than any self-consciousness I felt, and I did feel self-conscious, but not debilitatingly so.

Now, my fashion decisions in my late forties can be best

described by our poet laureate, Ariana Grande—"I see it, I like it, I want it, I got it"—because it's amazing what can happen when you delete the concept of "flattering" from your brain.

It's also amazing how quickly you can end up in debt.

I have spent *a lot* of money—more money than I have. I have lost control. I have been ashamed and worried. In 2018, I decided to do what I (apparently) do when something scares me: I wrote about it in a national magazine. All or nothing, baby! My theory is, if you have something potentially humiliating and definitely vulnerable and possibly hatred-inducing to say, do it in a public place. No day but today (to make people despise you).

I wrote the most honest version of my shopping habit as I could at the time, in *Cosmopolitan,* confessing, even, to the amount of money I had spent, which the publication put in the headline: "My Shopping Habit Cost Me $98,000 in 6 Months." Coming up with a specific number was a requirement of my editor's, so I was forced to look at my banking history and credit card statements in ways I hadn't before. I was forced to look at what I'd done. The figure, ninety-eight thousand dollars, included furniture and trips and therefore was a slight mischaracterization, I felt, but not enough to put up a fight. It's not like telling people I'd spent seventy-eight thousand on clothing in six months would prove that I *didn't* have a problem. The more important part was that to dig myself out, I was able to access investment accounts my parents had set up for me long ago, and they helped me on top of that. The most important part

was that the happy ending of the article—I stopped shopping!—
wasn't real or true, at least not for any sustained amount of
time.

After publication, a lot of people messaged to say they could
relate and were grateful I'd written the piece. A lot of people
commented online that I was spoiled and privileged (I agree);
they were absolutely incensed that my parents had helped bail
me out. I hadn't really gone broke after all, because I had a
safety net. I treated money as if it were the Monopoly kind because I could. I was not living paycheck to paycheck and at risk
of losing my home, so the whole thing felt a bit like role-play.
My anxiety was real, but it was born out of shame, not danger.

I know what you're thinking: Some people have real problems, and this is not one of them. I say the same thing to myself. But many of us who shop compulsively do it because of
other things (body grief, ADHD). My coping mechanism became its own problem, and I'm not being hyperbolic when I say
that sometimes I feel like I can't stop. Other than a brief period
after my wisdom teeth, when my affection for the Vicodin bottle scared me just a little, mounting credit card debt in my adult
life has been the closest I have ever felt to being out of control.
It took me until forty to become so unmoored. I guess that's
something?

I have a close friend who left New York to get away from
cocaine, and I understand this on a visceral level. But there is
no physical place for me to go to escape my drug. Well, that's a
lie. I could go to the woods. I could get off Instagram. I don't
want to, I guess is what I mean. I love shopping and clothing
and dressing up. Without them, I don't feel like myself.

This probably sounds so frivolous and gross. But it's not like Kim Kardashian with her diamond earring in the ocean and Kourtney droning, "People are dying, Kim." I'm not actually precious about the items themselves. I don't crumble if I tear or stain or lose things, which I do a lot because I am extraordinarily klutzy and absentminded. It's what the items signify, which is proof of life and crystal-clear projection of who I am at a given time. Decorating myself in something beautiful or cool or trendy instead of something bland and meant to blend me into the background means that I refuse to be sidelined or silenced. I want people to look at me, and I want to make sure that when they do, what they're seeing is an accurate representation.

After the *Cosmo* article, producers from a BBC podcast and an NBC daytime show and *Dr. Phil* reached out to see if I was interested in talking more about my sickness. *The Daily Mail* had a field day, mining my Instagram for photographic proof of my addiction. Comments on that article included, "A typical woman who can't spend it fast enough," and "Do people ever grow up? Good luck to any man that gets stuck with women like this." (Okay, already, I'll go out with you!)

I wondered if Buzz Bissinger had incurred such vitriol from readers after he wrote about his own shopping addiction in *GQ* a few years prior. Because I couldn't help but think that part of the fun people were having, part of the draw, was taking aim at the utter indecency of a woman who couldn't say no, who was out of control, even if she were very apologetically so.

I hadn't mentioned my deformity in the article. Should I have? Did I need to? Would it have made me seem like less of a dick? Is that the point of writing, to convince people that you're not a dick? Would I have offended people less if I'd offered up K-T as a sacrifice? It might have made people understand my habit or given them a reason to excuse me. But I don't think I was looking to be excused; I think I was looking to be held accountable but by people I didn't know, who couldn't actually hurt me when they decided to hate me or when I inevitably failed at rehabilitation.

And I did fail, repeatedly. Publication was meant to keep me in check, but it didn't. Each subsequent skyrocket of my credit card bill led to further depletion of my investments and self-worth. Every time I couldn't stop shopping was another humiliation, and I did not share these publicly. I would confide in one or two trusted friends that I was out of control again and didn't know what to do, and occasionally I'd even tell my parents, usually through tears while apologizing and ranting about being afraid I would end up like Grandma Rae. But I still didn't stop because I didn't want to. Yes, I was worried and yes, I was ashamed, but I still loved to shop. I could not stop chasing the high of acquiring things, because no other high in my life has ever come close, though it can have the fleeting feeling of fairy dust sparkle. That momentary joyous rush of a beautiful new garment and how it makes my body feel may be temporary, but it is unmatched.

Perhaps this all seems surprising: Someone deformed should want to hide her body, not decorate it. And sometimes I did. But I think my love of clothes comes from the same place that told me I would never join the vampire, I would never want to envision myself so bloody and broken that I would cease to exist, because what's the fun in that? Disappearing yourself means no longer having a body to dress. I am too conceited, too afraid of missing out, too garrulous, too Libran. I can't *not* express myself through fashion. It truly never felt like an option. Compulsion or not, I am happy about it.

My weird body ultimately, unwittingly elevated my style, or at least made it more interesting than my peers'. Because maybe the skintight disco-style pants with the side zip everybody was wearing sophomore year of high school would not fit no matter how big I bought them (if I could find them too big, which I couldn't), but the forgiving Moschino sweater in the Back Room at Loehmann's would, as would the stretchy Anna Sui dress from her boutique on Greene Street in Soho, far away from my provincial peers and their sad suburban weekends. All my clothes have always said "look at me" in one way or another, whether that's a pair of Celine ankle socks with norm-core orthopedic sandals (currently wearing those) or a Fashion Brand Company tank dress covered in hundreds of pink bows (it's sitting in my closet waiting for summer). I think that's a really good thing for someone who was born with a disorder that makes her body prone to standing out already. Grandiosity-wise, nothing feels off limits. I am not a person who has ever looked at something opulent or over-the-top or eye-grabbing or major or costumish or severe and thought I couldn't pull it off. I could *so* pull that off, if only the designer would make it in my size and shape and budget. Many did not and do not want to; those stupid self-defeating fuckers who don't want my fat, deformed dollars, to whom I say, Big mistake. Big. Huge. (And side note: For all the horror that fast fashion brings upon the world in terms of sustainability and human rights abuses, the one segment it helps are fat people. When your only bottom line is money, you understand that catering to larger bottoms means larger profits, and many fast-fashion brands have given people in bigger bodies their first opportunity to decorate themselves like a cake. Thrifting may be more righteous, but not everyone can do it.)

"All you K-T kids are so outgoing," a doctor once told a friend with K-T, and I've wondered: Is my spotlight-seeking and refusal to wear sad-sack clothes designed to make me disappear not in spite of my disorder but *because* of it? And does the answer matter?

There are days walking down the street feels like a political statement. There are days walking down the street just feels like walking down the street. When a thin woman in a conventional body puts on a short or formfitting dress and goes outside, she is putting herself in a vulnerable position for gobs of reasons. I—and anyone else deformed or disabled or fat or trans or blurry in any way—am putting myself in that same position of danger plus others. One thing that has made me feel safer is talking about my body. Ever since I stopped setting up myself as a terrible surprise to be revealed, ever since I stopped cloaking myself in layers of fabric meant to hide me, and chose to celebrate myself instead, I have felt better.

*I celebrate my body by hiking!* you may be thinking. *I cele-*

*brate it with Zumba!* Like, fine, sure, go for it. But that's not what I'm talking about. I'm talking about throwing an actual fucking party on your body. I'm talking about the way we announce ourselves to the world. Maybe you're not a clothing person—that's cool! Maybe you're a bold-eyeliner person or a crazy nail polish person or a giant-bow-at-the-top-of-your-head person. You can be anything you want (including none of those things—I'm all of them, which is why I used them as examples). What I'm saying is that, for me, decorating myself like I am a fucking present and forcing the world to look at me is and always will be the biggest rush ever, even though I don't get to choose the kinds of looks I get. If you are in an unconventional body, you must do a sort of risk assessment that is not fair but crucial if you're interested in harm reduction, and I strongly, strongly encourage you to do it. For me, when it comes to clothes, because I was indoctrinated early, and because I have already spent so much time contemplating risk, dressing how I want is almost always worth it.

I mentioned Jacob Riis beach in Queens earlier; my friends and I call it Fat Girl Beach. We mean it in the best way. We mean "Our Beach." We mean "No-Shame Beach." It is the antithesis (geographically, ethnically, spiritually) to the beaches of Long Island I grew up going to. Riis is where I relearned to wear a bikini (my two-piece stint in high school was short), because so many other women did. Annie helped me take the first step. She (say it with me now—*like so many of us*) also has a history with diet culture and decided to ignore the rule that says only certain bodies should be seen in a two-piece. Seeing her do it helped me do it. Seeing me do it helped Melissa do it. Seeing Melissa do it, I am sure, helped somebody else do it.

Here is my point: You don't need a special occasion to wear that gown or crown or latex catsuit. Getting out of bed is a special occasion, and you *could* be dead tomorrow (#coffin-talk). Make your life a party—but give yourself a party budget, like I didn't—and wear things that make you feel fucking spectacular, because you are.

# 8.

## Counterphobia Works, but Only for a Little While

At sixteen, I went back to Pitch Pine Woods for my fifth summer. I was going to be a junior counselor, which meant I would be away from home for a full eight weeks. My coworkers were a mix of other former campers and people in their twenties or older, authority figures turned peers in the space of eleven months.

When I woke up in the Catskills that first counselor morning, I was dizzy with panic. It wasn't better for its familiarity but worse because I thought I'd banished it permanently. Things went almost exactly the way they had just four years ago, when I'd arrived at twelve, which suddenly felt very recent: paralyzing nerves upon waking, racing thoughts. My anxiety improved throughout the day, just as it had the first year, but even that reassurance wasn't enough to make the mornings bearable.

Nothing could rumble my guts like a bright cloudless sky and freshly cut grass.

I'd seen the rumble in both my parents: My dad masks his in a way that makes him seem overconfident and aloof; my mom's radiates off her like a halo. I don't know why mine was such a surprise to everyone. Four years before, Marge Cohn had batted it away for as long as she could, then come up with a reason— my body—and said nothing else, like what I was supposed to do to make the feeling go away or how to sit with it without losing my mind. I was in the exact same spot, both literally and figuratively, as I'd been at twelve, only now it was more embarrassing because I was sixteen and supposed to be getting ready for the best summer of my life. I was going to have the most freedom I'd ever had, and teenagers are supposed to want freedom. I'd be drinking and smoking. Maybe I'd get *experience.*

So why was I planning escape routes? Why was I counting days? Turns out I hadn't slayed the dragon of anxiety all those years ago, I'd merely scared it back into its cave, where it rested and powered up. Now I'd had the audacity to come back and bang on the walls. "Me again! Bet you're not so tough this time!" Except she was—that dragon was a mad bitch who would no longer be ignored. But I was sixteen, and only babies were afraid of things. I did not want to be a baby.

The worst part of being a counselor was that we arrived a week before the campers, so there was no structure. I told anyone who would listen that I thought I might have made a mistake, that maybe I should leave, and none of my friends seemed to understand why a great open expanse of hours was so destabilizing. It was the time my peers would look back on as the best part of the summer—no work, all play—but that for me was lighter fluid on the flicker in my belly.

The second-biggest perk of being a counselor instead of a camper was that I was now allowed to use the phone, so I called my parents, repeatedly. They encouraged me to give it time, repeatedly. I said I would. That felt like—was—progress.

The biggest perk of going from camper to counselor in the period of a year was Roscoe's. Roscoe's was the townie bar down the road, where everyone went on their nights off; the camp had a van to take them (now us) back and forth, regardless of how old we were. I had known about Roscoe's since my first summer; our counselors went there on their nights off, and we looked forward to the last week of camp when everyone got the same night off, like an end-of-summer present. Only senior staff, who were closer to our parents' age, remained on the property. While our teenage minders were gone, senior staff would help us move our counselors' beds to the lawn or the bathroom or another bunk, and our counselors would be so drunk when they got home, they'd sleep wherever they could find a mattress. Senior staff would have their own fun with us once we fell asleep, drawing mustaches and giant eyebrows on our faces. It was the best feeling, all of us being in on the joke and the joke itself.

I had never gotten drunk before, and at sixteen, as I waited for the van alongside my twentysomething coworkers, I was nervous but in a good way, giddy. I was excited to drink, to go to a bar. Once we were there, somebody asked me what I wanted and I told them a screwdriver because I didn't know what people ordered at bars—I knew only not to order shots, which my mother had warned could *literally kill me.* I immediately felt light and giggly. By my second drink, my flip-flopping—should I stay or should I go?—was gone.

I was too young to know about bar promises. I was too inexperienced to sense the fleeting nature of vodka-fueled bravado.

"I'm going to stay," I happily told Seth, a slightly older camper turned counselor. "I want to tell my parents right now."

"I'll go with you," he said, and we walked down a block of the fast-asleep town to the nearest pay phone. It didn't occur to me that I might sound drunk, and it must not have occurred to my parents either, because they sounded happy. Maybe they didn't care whether I was drunk because they were just relieved to hear that I'd come to the right decision.

The next morning, the bad feeling was back, and worse, because I'd upped the stakes the night before by calling my parents and putting a period on the Should I Stay or Should I Go? conversation. I felt more trapped than before and couldn't manage it. I called them again from the main house and said *Get me out of here.*

A few hours later, here we were: me, my parents, girls' camp director Lori, and counselor Pam, who had worked at camp at least as long as I'd been going.

"You have to stay," Pam said. "I've been so excited for us to hang out."

"Just think about it some more." That was all of them—my mother, father, Lori, Pam. This seemed to be the prevailing directive anytime this happened—just think about it, just give it time—which for someone in the throes of an anxiety attack is like hearing, "Just feel terrible! It'll go away eventually, maybe!" It was the open-endedness that made me anxious to begin with, so when the supposed antidote was more open-endedness, it did not help.

I could tell that everyone was slightly exasperated with me, and I felt rushed. I wanted to stay. Or, maybe, I *wanted* to want to stay. I wanted to go back to Roscoe's. I wanted to be friends with twenty-year-olds. But my insides wouldn't cooperate. My insides were saying, *Run!*

"Just think about it. Just think about it. Just think about it."

All I was doing was thinking about it, so I didn't know how to think about it more. We stood in a loose rectangle on the wet grass, center of camp, the worst game of foursquare ever. I was trying to think about it; I really was. My mind was moving fast, playing out scenarios over and over, and each time I got to the end, whether I stayed or went my breath caught, because every decision felt like the wrong one. I was trying to slow my inhales and exhales, to keep myself calm, to do the things nobody had taught me to do yet. *Okay,* I thought finally, *ask me one more time and I'll stay. I can do this. Things will get better. Just ask me again and we'll finish this.* I don't know why I needed that, why I couldn't just say it, but I needed someone to ask me one more time. There was something ceremonious about it.

Lori looked at me like she'd read my mind, and I was ready. I was terrified but ready. I was going to try.

"You don't want to be here," she said. "It's over. You should go."

When we got home, my mother said, "You run from things," a factual assessment, not a cure, and it was something I already knew. People weren't supposed to be runners except for in the ways I wasn't, like for 5Ks. I could tell my parents were annoyed that I was home, both for me and for them.

Eventually I told my mom the reason I'd wanted to leave camp was all the drinking, and that softened her slightly. I supplied a lie to make my failure more palatable. Pressure around alcohol was an acceptable reason to leave; fleeing because of a terrible feeling you still could not name was not. Now that I was home, I did not want to be hated for being there, so I made a fictive offering in the hopes it would make my presence less irritating.

Suddenly I was on vacation with my parents, then scrambling to find a job on Long Island. It felt like a very long summer. The acute anxiety was gone, but it was replaced with a duller one, a steady thrum that was the worry I would always be like this, that I would have this feeling until I could prove to everyone that I was no longer a runner, which I might not ever be able to do.

I looked back on my last moments at Pitch Pine for a long time, that fork in the road in the Choose Your Own Adventure that was my life and thought, *This is where you missed the opportunity. This is where you fucked it up. You chose the wrong path and now it will always be harder to find your way back to the right one.*

It was the isolation that was the worst, the belief—so pervasive in the '90s, when nobody talked about mental health— that legions of people were Absolutely Loving Their Lives! and living without fear and the constant sense of anticipation in their throat, the infinitely compounding sandwich of desolation on top of nerves on top of desolation on top of nerves. (That sandwich has zero Points, maybe fewer, as anxiety is the only feeling that can steal my appetite.)

I tend to think of camp as my anxiety origin story, but of course it started long before. As a child, my frequent bedtime refrain as my mother tucked me in was "Mommy, I'm thinking of people dying," and I remember it vividly: a loop of all the people in my life I loved, dead, gone, and me alone in a vast, empty world. (Sleep tight!)

Though I didn't realize it for a long time, anxiety was the most ubiquitous feeling in my life. I kept repeating camp in different iterations that were all exactly the same. So many things that seemed easy for other people, that didn't seem to terrorize them with the prospect of forever-ness or no-way-out-ness, were hard for me. I present to you:

### A Short List of Things That Were Objectively Good or at Least Not Bad That Made Me Feel Like I Was Dying

—The summer before college was three straight months of panic, and I sought reassurance and common ground with everyone else getting ready to leave: "Are you nervous about going to school? Are *you*?" Of slightly older kids: "Were you worried when you first went to college? Were you scared?" No, no, no. Nobody else was nervous; everyone was eager to get there already. I was weird and absurd and defective for not being ecstatic to run from the grip of everything I knew into uncharted territory.

—My first trip to Europe at eighteen, on a tour, with my friend Meg. Everything about our English hotel freaked me out. The smell of it, the way the electrical outlets were different. I never thought I would miss American electrical outlets, but now I couldn't get over how comforting it would be to see one, or to find a sandwich that wasn't slathered in mayo and cheeses I couldn't identify. As soon as I landed in this country I'd been so excited to visit, I started counting the days until I could leave, a shrinking number I turned over in my brain whenever I needed a little bit of reassurance, which was always.

—My job at Lord & Taylor the summer after freshman year of college. I started every morning with a loud, violent anxiety attack, though I still didn't know to name it that. I called my mom as soon as I arrived most days, and she would sometimes drive out to talk me down because I didn't see how I could go on. I wanted to quit but didn't dare because I knew I'd be chastised for it, like I had been when I quit camp. I hadn't even picked Lord & Taylor in the first place; my mother put in an application for me one day while she was shopping, and when I got the job, saying no didn't feel like an option. One morning I was so out of control—the crying and ranting and not-being-able-to-breathe-ing, just steps away from the racks of clothes I was supposed to be replenishing and tidying—my mother told me later she thought I might hit her.

—My first months as deputy editor at *Time Out* in 2014. Every morning was the same: I'd be crying by the subway and cleaned up by the time I got to my desk. When I was promoted to editor in chief a year and a half later, I repeated the process, only worse this time because there was so much more pressure and responsibility and I had nobody to hide behind. I knew I would be exposed for the imposter and talentless hack I was. The weekend after I got the promotion, I sat on my bed hyperventilating and taking Xanax, absolute unmovable stone. I knew there was no way I could do the job and even less chance that I could do it well, but I also couldn't say no, because where would that leave me? I could kill myself or I could grit my teeth and try to do the job.

—My first weeks as executive editor at *Entertainment Weekly* in 2017. I hadn't been ready to leave *Time Out* (surprise, I loved being editor in chief), but when a job offer materialized, I decided it was better to leave the party too soon than too late. The move felt like a mistake instantly. It just wasn't a vibe fit, and in week one, I found myself crying in front of my editor in chief, which was humiliating. The only reason the weeks of unraveling didn't turn to months is that my excessive, unstoppable crying finally got me on antidepressants, something my psychiatrist had been suggesting for a while. I had resisted only because I'd never been diagnosed as depressed and didn't know antidepressants could treat anxiety, too. Zoloft made me flat and agreeable, which made the job tolerable, if not something I particularly enjoyed.

There's more. All my lists are endless-seeming.

The common denominator was a fear of being trapped someplace, literal or figurative: at college, in a hospital, in my body when it was racked with nerves, at a dinner I didn't want to be at, in a vacation house in the Hamptons, in a relationship with someone I no longer liked. If I accepted the job, what happened if I regretted it and wanted my old one back? If I dated that guy, what if I decided to get rid of him and couldn't? Sometimes being trapped looked like leaving; sometimes it looked like staying. It all felt terrible.

An issue for me is that I am good at many things (#conceited)—not always great, but at least good. I was a good student. I was a good athlete. I was good at so many things because I was a people pleaser who had trouble tolerating the feeling of others thinking I was not good. I had the proof of my goodness in the feedback, including from my supervisor at Lord & Taylor, who told me what a good salesgirl I was when I called her one final day while hyperventilating to say that I absolutely could not come back into the store.

Hearing that you are good at something that feels like it's killing you isn't encouraging. When people tell you you're good at something, they mean they think you're *effortlessly* good at it, but what they can't see is that you're putting in all of the effort all of the time while telling yourself that you're not putting in enough effort, which other people around you seem to agree with, because they keep suggesting that if you just put in even *more* effort, you could prevail over these things, but you have no more effort to give and already feel terrible about what a disappointment you are.

The summer after college graduation, 1998, was the big bad of paralytic depression, the one that is to this day a specter, a reminder of what could happen anytime, anywhere, without warning. I was twenty-one with twin degrees in English and journalism, both magna cum laude, and absolutely no more understanding of my mental health than when I was twelve and sobbing in front of Marge Cohn. Waiting it out was still my only coping mechanism, but when you have nothing bookmarked on the other side, nothing to quit, no destination to work toward, waiting it out is a permanent vacation in hell. Those structureless few days before the campers arrived my final doomed summer at Pitch Pine were my post-college life now, only worse, because the campers were never coming.

My college roommate Lauren was starting a graduate program in the fall. So were my friends Meg and Daniella and Ilana. Todd and John had secured their first jobs. Annie and Amy had one more year of college. I had been left behind, just as I always feared. I was back in my childhood bedroom staring at the Laura Ashley wallpaper and doing literally nothing. I had no hopes. I had no ambition. I was sleeping later and later. The only event in my calendar was going to the gym, which I did every day as a way to get out of the house, which no longer felt like home. Other than that, I saw no exit.

My parents alternated talking to me sternly about finding a job and ignoring me. Eventually, I could no longer tolerate the feeling of simultaneously being such an irritant and a disappointment, so even though the idea of getting up and going to a job every day terrified me, I started looking. I sabotaged the first couple of interviews—one at a privately owned glossy, the other at a fashion trade in a run-down office near Penn Station—because I could not imagine how I would ever get myself to these places and make myself stay. I told the owner of the trade that I had my sights set on bigger places, like *Elle* and *Vogue,* which wasn't true—I didn't have my sights set on anything. I told the editor of the glossy that I'd given his magazine only a cursory flip. He laughed and shook his head in a way meant to castigate me: "It really amazes me when people come in for interviews and haven't even read the product." *Yeah, well,* I thought, *what you don't know is that I'm trying really hard not to get this job.*

I spent one day volunteering for the New York Public Interest Research Group Fund—even unpaid work would at least be something—going door to door in Westchester asking people to donate money to fight pesticides. My shadow for the day said I was a natural. When I got back to the office, I was panicking. A lie formed itself: "I've been trying to decide between public service and journalism," I told my supervisor. That part was true, or had at least been partly so in college, when I was running Student Food Rescue and volunteering for other groups. "Today clarified for me that it's journalism." That part was obviously not true, but I still didn't know how to explain the feeling I was experiencing or why I was experiencing it. I didn't know how to say, "I'm having a lot of anxiety and this isn't the right choice for me now," because I didn't know I was having a lot of anxiety, I just knew that I was failing again. What I was thinking was, *I am weak and pathetic and weird but right now I just need to get the fuck out of here.*

Some days I would go to Barnes & Noble and search for guidance in the self-help section. Eventually my parents said I had to work for my dad's business a few days a week, which I did first from home and then from their Manhattan apartment, where at least I had room to breathe. I don't know if the work I did was any good and also knew it didn't matter: Its purpose was supplying me with something to do.

I kept looking. Though the idea of going to a job every day scared me—truly scared me, for reasons I still didn't understand—I knew I no longer had a choice and might as well try to find something that interested me.

Finally I got an internship at New York Women in Film and Television that for some reason didn't terrify me as much as everything else did. Maybe it was the tiny office, and the very small staff composed of only women, or the fact that I didn't have to go in every day, and that I got to see a lot of free movies. I was a good intern. NYWIFT hired me as a freelance development associate after the internship was done. In the fall I started a graduate program in creative writing at Emerson College.

Hot on the heels of my depressive post-undergrad episode—which loomed much larger than its actual length, six months—and desperate to never, ever repeat it, while I was getting my MFA, I was gripped by an idea: What if I ran *toward* the things that scare me? What if I did this indiscriminately? What's the worst that could happen: paralysis and the feeling that I would die? Been there, done that. Might as well be there, do it again and see what happens. My positive experience at NYWIFT bolstered me. Maybe if I made choices and then committed to them as if they were blood oaths, I could prevail over my terror through sheer force of will.

I was not as flip about it as I sound, but I was also determined. I did not want to finish grad school and be immobilized again. I told myself it was called manifesting, bitches, but it was actually called counterphobia (bitches). Instead of avoiding the things that scared me, I sought them out as a way of eluding the thing that *really* scared me: ending up back in that bed.

I applied to Emerson's LA summer internship program after my first year because it interested me a little bit and scared me a lot. I had wanted to study abroad during college, but my nerves would not let me go. Though the edge of the San Fernando Valley, where my apartment was, was not quite Paris or Amsterdam, going there accomplished the same feat: I was doing something that sounded theoretically cool but that I didn't *really* want to do. When I arrived to the Oakwood apartments at the foot of the Hollywood Hills, I sat on my twin bed in the room I would be sharing with a stranger, took a deep breath, and thought, *In sixty days, I can go home.*

Unwittingly, I started my counterphobic experiment in the place that rattles my nerves the most. I had never been to California before. Intellectually, I understood why people loved it and even why they liked Los Angeles, but there was something about it, an energy and vastness I couldn't quite name, that made it feel like the most alienating place I'd ever been. LA's persistent pleasantness was like a vise around my slippery, manufactured sense of calm—like one of those wibbly-wobbly self-inverting liquid-filled worms we children of the '80s used to play with—but I was determined to prevail over my feelings by making it the entire summer without trying to leave. And guess what: I succeeded, if success is the same as endurance. I made friends. I took a screenwriting class. I interned three days a week at a production company where they loved me and sent me off at the end of the summer with a cake, a tub of Coffee Bean & Tea Leaf vanilla powder, and a gift certificate to Barneys. (None of my friends in the program got end-of-summer presents from their internships.) I spent my days off at the beach or apartment-complex pool, which was populated by adult actors looking for work and child actors supporting their families. When I got back to New York, I remember feeling incredibly proud of myself for going, relieved to be home, and completely indifferent about whether I ever saw Los Angeles again. I had proved something to myself, which was the point.

Back at school, I started teaching intro lit and writing, which I enjoyed and was good at, but that was easy when my only other responsibilities were taking writing classes and hanging out with my friends. The end of my program was looming, and because I was still desperate not to leave any space for depression to creep back in, I decided I would seek out sections to teach as soon as I was back in New York with my degree, even though I wasn't entirely sure it's what I wanted. It didn't matter: Keeping myself busy, keeping the hours occupied, was my only goal. If you do not rest, anxiety can't find you. (I came up with this myself!) Anything that could keep me out of bed, whether it was something I wanted or I something I didn't, would do, and I couldn't always tell the difference. What used to be vigilance had turned to an always-moving-never-stopping. I decided that the best way to stay out of bed was spinning myself in so many directions at once, never slowing down, so that I couldn't even see the bed, which meant I couldn't possibly find it, except very occasionally, by accident.

Back in the city at twenty-five, I immediately hated everything about teaching other than the actual time in the classroom, which wasn't much. I loved engaging with students, but I hated the isolation of an adjunct life. I hated the self-doubt that crept in, making me wonder how I could possibly be qualified to teach anything to anybody. I hated the lack of glamour in commuting to Queens and Brooklyn colleges and returning home with towering stacks of papers to grade when other people my age and younger were working at fancy magazines. I still had anxiety, a lot of it, but it was not paralyzing, which had become my one and only benchmark of success. Was I able to get to work in the morning? Yes! Great. Carry on.

After a few years of teaching, I decided to take another risk: I told my chairperson I would not be signing on for another semester and started applying to other jobs. Another impulsive decision, made to ensure that I kept making decisions and did not remain stagnant.

When I got a job I didn't want, as a receptionist at a literary agency, I called my mom from the M23 in tears and told her between gasps, "I'll do it for a year. It'll be fine."

"How are you going to do *this* for a year?" She meant that taking a job that upset me this much was obviously not a good idea. I was so confused.

All those decades of being a disappointment for not sticking things out—how was I supposed to know there was another option? How was I meant to tell the difference between a risk worth taking and a situation that was simply not a good fit? How was I supposed to know when perseverance was the answer and when it was acceptable to bow out gracefully? What the fuck was going on?

But I was relieved, because I needed someone else to tell me it was okay to turn down the job, regardless of my reasons. I was crying. That was a stop sign. I would heed it. Someone else—and not just anyone else, my mother—said so. The thing I had missed about the Choose Your Own Adventure fable I told myself for so long was the choice part.

I interviewed for a reporter job at a Queens newspaper and spent most of the interview trying to explain why I was not qualified. The editor did his best to persuade me that I was. I took the edit test. I made it to the next round of interviews. Bolstered by my new knowledge that I was allowed to say no to things, I emailed to respectfully take myself out of the running. I still believed I was not qualified (reader, I was qualified), but I also realized I did not want this job. I was getting better at making decisions instead of waiting to be acted upon. Eventually I got into a groove and found jobs I wanted to do, at least a little bit. I worked at that vanity mag where my bosses were nuts. I got hired as a freelance copy editor at *Life & Style*, then went full-time, then ran the desk, then became managing editor. I had jobs that didn't feel like they were killing me, that I went to every day successfully. I never believed I would be able to, and then suddenly I was. Well, suddenly after years and years of trying.

Trial and error. Case by case. That's how I got there. It was imperfect and long but effective. And no decision—right or wrong—killed me. I tried to remember that.

There's that "do one thing that scares you every day" mantra, and it's a nice thought to stick on a mug, but only if you make some addendums: First, the thing that scares you doesn't have to be huge. Maybe it's leaving the house. Maybe it's getting out of bed. Second, if it scares you to the point that you feel traumatized, then absolutely do not do it every day. Not yet. Not now. Third, not everybody has the luxury of the first and second points, because those points take privilege, and if your livelihood depends on doing something that happens to scare you, there may be no way around it. (I guess it would be a very big mug.)

If you're like me, you may not always know whether or not you want to do something, and "something" could be "take the job" or "go to the party" or "order Chinese for dinner." You may have so many conflicting feelings about it—and so much noise in your head thanks to future-tripping every possible outcome of every possible choice, plus a shame hangover from years of avoidance—that you just can't tell. When that happens, any decision you make will probably feel a little bad.

If you're like me, you may be so disconnected from your own physiological reactions to things that you're sometimes unable to tell the difference between what you feel and what you think you feel or what you *want* to feel. For example: I smoked weed every now and then from sixteen to my thirties. As often as not, I'd freak out once the high kicked in, but for some reason I thought of my freakouts as one-offs. I never put it all together, that's how out of tune my brain and body were. Over and over I would smoke pot and feel paranoid, edgy, nervous, sometimes thinking I was dying, sometimes thinking I was having a psychotic break, occasionally worried that this was the moment I was tipping over into bipolarity like my grandmother and great-grandmother. And still I'd never think, *Maybe pot's not the drug for me*. The math would have been simple if I'd tried to do it, but because I hate math and didn't want to, I miscalculated. I thought something was true and one day realized that none of the proof from my own experience backed it up.

So many years of instinct-denying, it rubbed off everywhere: I was hungry but wasn't supposed to be. I wasn't ready for boys but was supposed to be. I was anxious, but anxious was not cool or okay and therefore I should not be anxious and would not be anxious and could not be anxious and wasn't anxious.

I could talk about my anxiety at twelve or seventeen or twenty-two or thirty-five; the important part is where I am speaking from, which is now, in my late forties, post-anxiety. By "post" I don't mean that I no longer have anxiety (it's probably pretty evident that I do!). What I mean is that I coexist with it now after years of trying other things. I have learned to live with it instead of worrying that I will never shake it. I won't shake it—it's part of me—but it isn't paralyzing anymore. And I've given up the experiment of making my life one big exposure-therapy session just to be able to say I could.

I can't say whether my body and my anxiety are connected. Did my fear of being trapped originate in my skin? Marge Cohn assumed that and at some point made me wonder if she was right. When you're born with a body as weird as this one, it's easy to assume that everything and anything that afflicts you must be tied to it. It's the perfect fall guy. I suppose my body could be a factor as much as anybody's anything is a factor in making them something else. I grew up with a dad who intimidated me and a mother who yelled "Help!" in her sleep. I have friends on all manner of SSRIs, SNRIs, and benzos who didn't grow up like that and also don't have Klippel-Trenaunay. If my body is part of it, it is just that: part. Assuming the most obvious answer to be the right one—my body is responsible for my anxiety—is a child's way of understanding mental health. It lacks depth and texture. I had to find that out for myself, because to my parents I wasn't anxious, I was a runner; to Marge Cohn, I *was* anxious but for a singular reason; to all the people who saw me counterphobically prevailing over things just to say I could, I probably seemed strong and fearless. I am all of those things. I am none of those things. The full picture of my anxiety is much more complex.

# 9.

## *What if Instead of Syndromes and Disorders We Called Them Cherries on Top?*

got the K-T diagnosis at birth, or a little bit after. It was easy to spot because I looked different from other babies. Even if the doctors hadn't known exactly what to call my affliction—that happens to people with Klippel-Trenaunay, sometimes it takes years to get the right diagnosis—at the very least they would have known I had *something*, because newborns with giant birthmarks and misshapen backs and different-sized legs don't have nothing. It's easy to spot the so-called defects and deformities and disappointments when they affect your appearance, especially on little-girl babies.

I got what I think of as the most important—or at least most eye-opening—diagnosis in my mid-forties, when I sought it out for myself: attention deficit hyperactivity disorder. I didn't believe it at first. Whoever named antidepressants did a bad job, but whoever named and then marketed attention deficit hyperactivity disorder did a worse one. ADHD never occurred to me because I am not a rambunctious little boy who likes to climb things.

Melissa is one of the very few women I know who got an ADHD diagnosis in childhood, so when she flagged mine, I listened. We were living together during the pandemic, and such close, constant proximity made her notice things: I was always getting up to fetch something in another room, then forgetting why or what. I would pop commitments into my calendar for the wrong day or month. I would get a particular kind of fidgety at night that I always attributed to my anxiety or quirkiness and would have to move around the room to get the energy out of my body. I was bad at sleeping.

I was skeptical of ADHD but curious enough that I mentioned it to my psychiatric nurse practitioner, Connie, whom I was now seeing for my SSRIs. Connie thought actually, yes, it did seem like I might have ADHD. We did a test. It confirmed what was becoming increasingly obvious.

ADHD is harder to spot than K-T, but maybe we should ask ourselves why. Finding out I had it—even finding out there was a *possibility* I had it—opened up another door I didn't know was there. (So many hidden doors; who knew life was like Narnia?) Maybe there was nothing wrong with me. Maybe the world just wasn't designed for people like me. Instead of spending so much time trying to squish my square-peg brain (and body, while we're at it) into a round-hole world, what if the world did some shapeshifting and tried to meet me halfway?

I had accepted most past diagnoses with stoicism and one with delight: the academic underperformance due to childhood trauma that my therapist Marilyn had given me years ago. But what if it wasn't that? Or what if it wasn't *only* that? What if we'd misidentified what the trauma was? Maybe the trauma was having the type of brain that this type of world is not built for and butting up against that frustration again and again.

I worried as much as I did because I failed so many of society's tests. In elementary school, I forgot books daily and had to be driven back to try to locate a custodian to unlock my classroom. Every report card had one glaring Not Satisfactory for talking too much. I was constantly making what my teachers deemed careless mistakes. I was always in trouble for my messy room but had absolutely no idea how to make it not messy. One day I proudly invited my mom in—"Come see! I cleaned my room!"—and I watched her elation turn to anger as she discovered that I had simply put everything in the closet. I didn't know that was cheating. It was the only way I could come up with to succeed. In high school chemistry, my teacher's rule was that you kept taking the midterm until you passed; it took me three tries. I accidentally double- or triple-booked friends, which resulted in (at best) uncomfortable configurations of people who wouldn't have otherwise spent time together or (at worst) my having to tell someone that I had screwed up and could no longer do the thing I had committed to because I was the worst person on the planet and if they couldn't forgive me I would understand.

As an adult, my eyes glazed over during work meetings with CEOs and COOs and analytics people as they talked to me of EBITDA and SEO and ROI and CTR and KPIs and UGC and other acronyms I barely understood and could not care less about, even when I was the editor in chief and therefore the one who was supposed to care the most; I became adept at nodding at the right times and taking notes to give the illusion of interest and understanding. I once showed up at a Miami hotel insistent that I had made a reservation, snippy with the front desk attendant when she told me I actually hadn't. I once showed up at a Napa hotel insistent that I had made a reservation and was told that yes, I had, but for the same day I'd booked it. I once showed up to a party and found that I'd accidentally slipped my giant cordless landline instead of my mobile into my bag, and was at least relieved to get some comedy fodder from it, whipping out the phone repeatedly over the course of the night to say, "Hey, does anybody need to make a call?" It took me around twenty years, on and off, to write this book.

How had we missed it? How had my mother, an educator for more than thirty-five years, an unequivocally excellent teacher who could spot a learning disability or teenager in need from a mile away, never picked up on it? But nobody did. And when I say nobody, I mean nobody, for so many neurodivergent women, for decades, including my mother; everybody missed hers, which is probably why she missed mine. We were the same. We were smart but flighty and doing twelve things at once and making too many plans and canceling and feeling bad about canceling and zoning out and overcommitting and regretting and perpetually buzzing with an aura of electricity and always, always losing our keys. We were in a perpetual state of fatigue. We couldn't make the piles of clothing go away. We sometimes seemed ditzy, even though my mom is, alongside my dad, one of the smartest people I know. (Admittedly, she and I both sometimes use miscalculations about us to our advantage, playing dumb and letting others—usually men—underestimate us to get what we want.)

ADHD is, it turns out, why I'm good at so many things. ADHD is why I'm bad at so many things. I fixated on the bad before I knew what to call it. My mistake-making turned into vigilance, which turned into worry, which turned into anxiety.

I was hesitant to try Adderall, mostly because I worried that speed would tweak my nerves. I didn't know that someone with a neurodivergent brain would respond differently. Connie gently prodded me. It could help, she said. She was right. Adderall made me focus. It gave me a kind of clarity I'd never experienced. It helped me write. It helped me organize my fridge. It made me want to shop less. Adderall quieted my brain like Wegovy did. (Shut up, brain!)

The drugs are alike in the way they help me adjust to a world that is not amenable to me. As with Wegovy, it would be better if the world were more elastic than it is, less hung up on diagnoses and particular ways of thinking and doing and being and more open to the idea that everybody's bodies and brains and experiences and likes and dislikes and tactics and habits are different and different is fine, there is no hierarchy, it's all a straight, value-free line. But the world is not like that. I could pretend it is or accept reality and do the things that make my life easier—complications and all. I take the antidepressants. I take the Wegovy. I take the Adderall. When I feel like I need to, I take the Xanax. Yes, I take a lot of drugs, but guess what:

I'm a calmer, happier person than when I was not taking the drugs. It's just chemistry adjustment. I may have flunked my chem midterm twice, but even I know that. The drugs aren't the important part, really; the important part was the discovery phase that led me to them.

A late ADHD diagnosis brought lots of emotions. Sadness for the kid who could have been helped but wasn't. Anger over the potentially missed opportunities. Elation for the adult that finally had the master key to decipher her life. Stupefaction that so many grown-ups failed so miserably. Empathy for those grown-ups because some of them were failed, too. Confusion because things I thought were personality traits are actually just really common characteristics for someone with ADHD. Gratitude for all the gifts I've come to learn are at least potentially related to my supposed deficit: my creativity, clear-headedness in a crisis, energy, curiosity, outgoingness, humor, ability to explain things really, really well even if sometimes I overexplain and use more words than I need to and go on a little too long and can't help it even when I can tell that everybody wants me to move on already, Jesus, does she ever stop talking, we get it.

I had one very early diagnosis that set my life on a certain course, then got another very late that helped me course correct. In between I did okay, mostly because I was lucky and (like most women and especially most women with ADHD) good at pretending and masking and pushing through even when things were hard and I didn't know why. I was set up from a very early age to soldier on, so that's what I did, with everything.

What a diagnosis of anything means is only important in

terms of what it means for you. The much more important part is understanding that nothing about you—not your body, not your brain, not your feelings—is wrong. You are just you. And if the world is not designed for you or accepting of you or amenable to you, that is the fault of the world.

# Word Search:
## ADHD Secret Symptoms Edition

L earning about my own ADHD has been a world shaker. Things I thought were flaws or personality traits or attributes of my star sign or, yes, trickle-down effects of K-T, are actually symptoms of neurodivergence. Those symptoms led to lots of things that non-ADHDers don't necessary struggle with (or at least don't struggle with because of this). Hidden below are words related to ADHD. Give finding them a whirl! And if you have a short attention span, feel free to take lots of breaks, leave it unfinished, or never even start.

```
F  I  D  G  E  T  Y  L  O  S  I  N  G  S  T  U  F  F  Y  E
U  Y  Z  E  S  I  S  Y  L  A  R  A  P  N  N  W  M  Y  N  T
O  T  D  T  E  X  T  U  R  E  I  C  K  D  S  K  K  D  E  J
V  F  O  R  G  E  T  T  I  N  G  A  T  E  U  B  L  D  P  T
E  O  V  E  R  S  P  E  N  D  I  N  G  C  L  E  A  I  E  P
R  S  I  N  T  E  R  R  U  P  T  I  N  G  S  C  H  S  E  A
S  O  E  W  F  Z  K  E  K  F  F  S  U  S  E  O  Y  O  X  Z
H  J  J  L  E  R  G  N  I  K  C  I  P  C  B  T  P  R  P  L
A  X  K  B  I  E  A  R  N  F  V  R  A  B  H  L  Y  G  I  Y
R  S  V  I  G  P  A  G  Z  Q  E  P  Y  G  E  Y  V  A  I  R
E  F  T  N  B  F  R  W  E  F  S  S  I  P  V  P  M  N  R  D
T  O  S  G  J  C  H  I  A  T  L  L  Q  Z  D  F  I  Y  N
R  R  T  E  T  S  M  C  A  U  F  E  F  Y  E  O  L  Z  K  U
E  G  E  E  A  Y  E  L  T  H  A  I  E  N  D  B  U  A  A  A
X  E  U  A  N  S  O  S  J  S  C  D  E  U  C  V  S  T  L  L
A  T  G  T  G  P  H  X  I  M  Q  P  M  D  C  Z  Q  I  F  T
R  T  I  I  E  N  V  N  E  U  O  P  L  H  M  Y  M  O  Z  E
M  I  T  N  N  L  G  Z  P  N  R  A  I  N  M  O  S  N  I  W
S  N  A  G  T  R  I  N  U  F  Z  B  O  R  E  D  O  M  G  V
J  G  F  E  S  E  V  I  T  I  S  N  E  S  Z  B  Y  Z  H  T
```

WORD LIST

| | | | | |
|---|---|---|---|---|
| BINGE EATING | TANGENTS | TEXTURE ICK | OVERSHARE | SENSITIVE |
| BOREDOM | FATIGUE | T-REX ARMS | UNOPENED MAIL | WET LAUNDRY |
| BRUISES | FIDGETY | HOBBY SLUT | OVERSPENDING | PEOPLE PLEASING |
| CHAIR PILES | FLAKY | INFO DUMP | PARALYSIS | DISORGANIZATION |
| FLIGHTY | INSOMNIA | PICKING | ENDLESS PREFACES | FORGETTING |
| FORGETTING | INTERRUPTING | RAGE | SPACE CADET | LOSING STUFF |

# 10.

## Do Not Go Missing to You

got my first tattoo at forty-one. After I filled out the paper-work and waited my turn, my mind was a news ticker running the same alert over and over: *After this, you will no longer be a person without tattoos. You will be different. You will forever be changed.*

It was a defensive response, a body protection. It was a warning that I might end up feeling trapped inside my own skin and there would be nothing I could do about it. I realized later it was also a reassurance: Being forever changed can be a good thing if you're the one making the choice to do it.

Let's get one thing straight right away: I am not telling you to get a tattoo. I am not saying that if you get one something magical will happen. I'm saying that the magic, for me, happened right before the decision itself.

Jewish girls don't get tattoos. Girls who aren't super cool or hip or thin or young don't get tattoos.

Tattoos are trashy. They degrade your body. They cheapen you.

These are things I used to tell myself. Except it turns out that all it takes to be the kind of person who gets tattoos is getting a tattoo. And all that changes once you've gotten one is that you have one. When you've gotten one because you wanted one, that is self-determination. Tattoos do not impact your worth any more or less than a lost or gained pound ever did, than the number of men you kissed ever did. The value of skin does not depreciate with wear. How you feel about being tattooed is the only thing that matters if you are the one getting the tattoo.

My great-aunt Fortuna, my mother's mother's sister, was a Turkish-born Sephardic Jew who spoke English, Spanish, French, and Ladino and interjected and ended conversations with incantations my cousins and I could only loosely translate: "Que te vea novia" I understood to mean that she wanted to see me as a bride (*lo siento*, Auntie!); the Arabic "mashallah" was something like "God willing," the Sephardic version of "poo poo poo" and "toi toi toi" and "knock on wood." "Saludozos" is the Ladino equivalent of *l'chaim* and translates literally to "to our health!" (When my family clinks glasses, we just say, "Health!") "Que no me manques" was Auntie's most frequent refrain, a Spanish one, and I knew only that it signified her care for me and that I should answer with "love you" or "you too" or something else expressing warmth and gratitude.

What it means literally is, "You shouldn't be missing to me."

"Mancar" is an obscure Catalonian verb that means "to lack." "Que no me manques" was Auntie's way of saying that she wanted me to always be with her. That I shouldn't be lost to her. That I shouldn't be lost. That I shouldn't let others make me that way. That I should be true to myself, once I figured out who that was. That I should mark it down in permanent ink.

I took some liberties—Auntie would absolutely not be happy about my having a tattoo—but I think it's an accurate adaptation.

Deciding to get a tattoo was a decision I made for myself and only for myself. I spent months researching artists and contemplating placement. I chose JonBoy because his fonts were dainty, celebrities liked him, his wait list was long, he tattooed out of the well-known shop Bang Bang, and he was expensive.

The actual session was short—I spent more time waiting for the appointment than on the table—and the needles nearly lulled me to sleep. Afterward, I felt blasé about what I'd done in the absolute best way. I looked at my now marked left triceps in the mirror—QUE NO ME MANQUES in two stacked lines—and said, "Cool."

"Be careful," JonBoy warned me with a laugh, "they get addictive."

Three weeks later I got my second tattoo. This time I found the artist by scrolling through Instagram and picking a premade design out of a book of flash art. I ascribed meaning to the abstract swirl of hearts with an eye at their center afterward, deciding it would ward off evil.

Forty-one years, reticence, trepidation, and all the research before surrendering my skin to something I was *pretty sure* I wanted. Then weeks after that, I picked a design with all the thought you give to deciding which shampoo to use today and produced my forearm without blinking. By forty-two, I had ten. As I write this, at forty-seven, I have eighteen—on my arms, fingers, and ankle—less than five years after my first. I have a block-letter tribute to my family's matriarchs: MARY, RHODA, RAE, FORTUNA. On my finger, I have a script "chutzpah." I have tulips and roses and one "Mashallah." I have hand-poked finger jewels and a "BRUJA." I have a teeny-tiny wishbone to commemorate the one I choked on while eating paella with my parents and Melissa.

Every appointment is more or less forgettable. I don't get nervous. I don't squirm. I don't ever go, "Uh-oh, maybe that was a mistake." After the artist is done, I get up, look in the mirror, say, "I love it," and leave, even when I occasionally don't love it. (My one foray into color tattoos left my forearm marked with what was supposed to be a pale-pink oval gem but looks more like a melanoma or an anus.)

The speed at which I've collected ink probably seems a little compulsive (surprise surprise); every new photo I post on Instagram garners a flurry of comments from friends and family that say different versions of "*Another* one?" A particularly obnoxious acquaintance offered this sage observation: "You realize you've just replaced your shopping addiction with a tattoo addiction, right?" (I'm still a shopping addict, dick, so joke's on you! Well, I guess it's on me, too. Hahahahaha. Anyway.)

I suppose it'd be easy to view my rapidly inked-up body

through the lens of a cosmopolitan midlife crisis, but I prefer to think of it as an awakening.

Before tattoos, my aesthetic rebellions were always of the reversible sort: bleach in my hair, holes punched all over my ears and in my nose. I used to stare enviously at people with ink, specifically lithe-armed Brooklyn women dotted in designs, and think, *Man, they look cool,* with that familiar invisible "tsk-tsk" hanging over it. What a pity that I could not be like them. But I couldn't, because my sense of self had never been so fixed. I chalked it up to a fear of commitment, a fickleness I couldn't shake. I even hid behind that myth about not being able to be buried in a Jewish cemetery, despite feeling the self-defeating prospect of planning one's life around death (even though, I know, I seem to spend a lot of time doing that).

In retrospect, it's clear that my body never felt mine enough to do something so permanent with—and why would it? My parents, the surgeons, the vampire, the Weigher Ladies, the men I dated—I was theirs, I wasn't mine. I strived to be whatever version of myself they demanded without ever stopping to ask what version I wanted to be or just was.

Tattoos have made me less precious about my body. Or, realizing that I wanted to get a tattoo—instead of just admiring them on other people and regretting that I could not join them—made me realize I had already become less precious. Because here's the thing: Even so-called "good" bodies change. Of course they do. Botox and diets and face-lifts and shapewear and other supposed time stoppers wouldn't exist if they didn't. But you don't have to be an unwilling participant in that change. You don't have to wait to be acted upon in a way that feels negative. You can actively, positively, purposely change yourself. And in that way, because I'm the one who is deciding what to do with my body, it means that I realize it is the *most* precious thing. Bodily autonomy: You don't need a weird deformity, especially not now, to know how crucial it is. (Who's making the bumper stickers?)

As a child, I dreaded the needles that came with liposuction, a procedure meant to make me more palatable to others. At thirty-eight, suddenly overwhelmed that I was middle-aged, I spent thousands of dollars on fertility treatments, piercing my stomach repeatedly for weeks because of a ticking clock on children it turns out I didn't even want. With HCG and Wegovy, I did it—ambivalently do it—to make myself smaller. With tattoos, I go willingly toward the needles for myself, and for a much happier reason: because you don't adorn things you don't love, and you don't embellish that which you hope will disappear. I've fallen in love with tattoos because they are the physical reminder that my body is not a democracy, it's a dictatorship, and I am the head bitch in charge. It is a reminder that skin is just skin, and nothing else changes about me when I mark it. That's not true when somebody else decides that you need to be marked. When someone else makes the decision, they are taking something from you.

I love all my tattoos, but that first one will always be my favorite: Do not go missing. Do not get lost. Do not lose yourself. Do not. It's a nice reminder, even though its placement behind my elbow means I can't actually see it. I don't need to. I fight every day to make sure I won't ever forget it, and it gets easier and easier with age, in ways big and small.

If I'm tired and I want to go home, I go home.

If a friend asks for plans and I realize I don't feel like seeing that friend or doing the thing he wants us to do, I say no.

If someone offers me a job and I don't want it and I can afford to turn it down, I do.

Instead of trying to please everyone else, I think about what I gain by prioritizing others and their opinions of me.

I ask myself if my decision will hurt anyone else and whether I have chosen the path of least resistance just because it's the most pleasant for everyone else. What does always acquiescing to your own detriment get you in the end? Not much. Not even the memory of your goodness, I bet.

Turns out there's nothing particularly rewarding about being easy or good. I would rather be good to myself. I would rather be a little selfish in the purest sense of that word. I would rather not go missing to me while in the pursuit of making myself easily found by others. In fact, I want to be harder to find. I want to be hidden except to the people who work very, very hard to discover me.

# 11.

## *Just Swim*

There are days, even now, at forty-seven, when my body shocks me. There are days when I do not feel safe inside it because I can't control the world around me, and there are still bastards out there roaming free. (If anything, the bastard population in the world seems to have increased over the past few years.) There are days I look at my face and find it unrecognizable thanks to time and gravity and light and mood and everything else that can impact human skin. I can catch myself at an angle I wasn't expecting and think, *Whoa.*

Or I can get stuck in my imagination, unable to picture next-life fantasy goals in a body like mine. I want to know what it feels like to be thrown in the air by a pas de deux partner. I want to do a split. I want to run a marathon. I want to sit at a piano bench like Tori Amos or Alicia Keys or Lady Gaga or Taylor Swift and have it look sexy and cool. I could physically do this last one—sit down at a piano and make someone listen to me sing and play (no one would enjoy this), but I can't *picture* it. Not in this body. In my head, when I see myself writhing around a Steinway bench, my back is flat. Even though I have come as far as I have—and it is very, very far—I still have a pang of "No, not with your body" when I picture these things. Doing them in this body still sometimes feels silly. I am working on it. I will never stop working on it.

I may not love myself all the time, I may not always think, *Lookin' good, hot stuff!* but I never think, *You don't deserve to live* or *You are gross* or *How do you ever even leave the house?* That wasn't always true.

Bear with me for a sec: If someone were staring at you on the street, really staring, what would you do? You would confront them, maybe. You would say, "Hey, buddy, got a staring problem?" At the very least you would roll your eyes or cross the street or in some other way absent yourself from the situation, because being stared at is weird. And yet we spend so much of our lives making ourselves palatable to the gaze of others. Why? Why do we do that? If that's not a lose-lose proposition, I don't know what is.

I thought my body was an asterisk, but I need to asterisk that. Thinking it didn't make it so, which is good news, because it means I never had to undo it, not really. You know how Dorothy realizes home is where the heart is or that she never left Kansas or whatever it is that she figures out after her trip to Oz? It's sort of like that. I had the luck of a relatively solid foundation, so after putting in the requisite wasted time hating myself and thinking that my body was everything or nothing, I realized it's neither. It just is.

The bastards may be emboldened, but so am I. So can you be.

It'd be easy to think I am everything I am (and am not) because of this rare disorder that I happened to be born with. I used to get angry at my body because I felt it precluded me from knowing my true self. Without this body, I wondered, if I had two legs that matched, would I be an entirely different sort of person? Would I be someone like the vampire or the frat boy or the man who said I didn't live up to his expectations?

But that logic is faulty and falls apart quickly on closer inspection, because none of us can separate out any one part of ourselves and still be ourselves. People are wholesale, not retail (ooh, shopping!), and my desire to know who I would be without my body is self-defeating and more of the same old magical thinking that locked me in a box for so long. Asterisk, asterisk, asterisk. Sometimes I wonder if K-T has been an easy way for me to separate myself from other people and maybe even feel a little bit superior. *There, there, dear,* I'd think, *you don't really understand, but then, you've never had to.* More margin flitting, more hydroplaning. It was a great way to stop myself from sinking my teeth into life for a very long time.

Here's something I know in my bones now: I would hate the vampire and the frat boy and that man I went on one date with even if I had two legs that matched and a flat back.

I want you to hate them too, but I can't teach you how, I can only hope that you'll learn. In dribs and drabs. Partly that's because I don't entirely know how I did it, I know only that I always wanted to. It's difficult to even recall the before. I have to force myself really hard to remember that there was a time when I wouldn't get up from the table at a restaurant to use the bathroom without putting on my coat—that's how foreign an action it feels to me now. Back then, it would have felt as foreign—and impossible—to imagine that I would ever *not* do that. The biggest factors for me have been age and experience. So while I want my book to give you a shortcut, I can't promise that it will. You have to get to a point in your life when you realize you can either hate yourself or love yourself, and then you must decide—*decide,* every goddamned day—that loving yourself means a happier life. You have to think you're worthy of that. You have to surround yourself with people who agree and remind you.

You have to intrinsically believe that one in 100,000 doesn't have to be a curse; one in 100,000 can also mean you're rare and precious, like a gem. (And not the one on my arm that looks like an anus.)

You have to want to go AWOL from the Bastard Brigade, even if you willingly enlisted to join the people who wanted to hurt you. The self-hatred I experienced felt real, but it was make-believe. I loved myself; I was rooting for me. I always knew that I deserved better than the vampire. I don't know why I knew—good parenting, an intrinsically strong sense of self, an extroverted need to be in the spotlight, always—but I knew I was not down for the count.

You have to realize that the playing field is not level and that if you are in a marginalized group because of your race or gender or health, it will be harder for you, and that sucks, so you have to join the fight to dismantle the institutions that keep things that way while protecting your heart, mind, body, and time. You have to try to vote out of office anyone who does not have your humanity in mind. You have to rally against anyone who thinks anything other than autonomy is the right choice for a body.

You have to witness people who've gone before you on the journey and come out the other side. (Hi.) More than anything you have to *want* to love yourself (or even want to want to). If you have that, you're already on your way.

Of course it doesn't mean you don't have bad days. It doesn't mean your path won't sometimes be littered with people whose entire reason for being is disrupting your progress. I wish I could do something about them, but I'm more concerned about you (and me). It doesn't mean you won't be tempted to change yourself. It just means that your view of the world and your own place in it shifts, maybe slightly, maybe more than slightly. It means you realize (in a good way!) how short life is and what a colossal waste it is to fritter it away by constantly critiquing yourself. It doesn't mean you won't need some help along the way. For me, it means this:

### An Incomplete List in No Particular Order of Progress I've Made, Stuff That No Longer Gets Me Down, and Things I Say and Do That I Wouldn't Have Before

—I fire doctors.

At some point I stopped going to doctors who shamed me, like the one who, after seeing my weight, told me I must really like eating cake (are there people who don't like eating cake?); and the one who, upon seeing my forty-pound loss, said, "That's really good. Don't gain it back," ensuring that I would. Even in the realm of medical bigotry, I was on the lucky side: There are fat people who are refused treatment because of their size and nothing else. They are simply too much of a risk, these doctors say. The exceptions are very dangerous procedures that are in service of making the patient thinner, like bariatric surgery. Fatphobia math. Now I get rid of doctors who don't meet my standards instead of trying to live up to theirs. They are dead weight.

—I don't date jerks.

Life is *much* better when you're not dating jerks. It seems obvious when you hear it, and yet so many of us have dated so many jerks. I bet you can think of friends dating jerks right now. Maybe *you're* dating a jerk right now. I don't do it anymore. Your body, your choices, of course, but you really shouldn't either. Which means, as a corollary:

—I listen to my instincts, even when they're muffled.

I see red flags for what they are, and I do not ignore them. It doesn't matter if they are faded or so far off I could convince myself they're a different color or maybe not flags at all. I abide them. If I am trying extraordinarily hard to make something work that doesn't seem to want to—a relationship, a job— instead of forcing it, I ask myself whether something good and right for me should take this much work. When I get that funny feeling in my stomach or that little itch at the back of my brain, I take a minute and examine it. I trust it. I trust my own ugly guts.

—I remove from my life anyone who dims my light.

Think of your people: friends, family, anyone you spend time with voluntarily. Do they lift you up? Do they celebrate your successes? Do they extend a hand when you fall? Do you feel good when you're around them? Do you feel a natural desire to have only good things happen to them because you know the feeling is mutual? Do they never, ever, *ever* make you feel bad about your body or encourage you to change it? Removal is admittedly a final resort. It comes after polite discussion, then impolite discussion, then notice of impending eviction. (I am also an advocate for quiet quitting expired friendships.) With so many other people in the world happy to take you down a peg, why would you let people like this into your life willingly? Begone, negative Nancys and passive-aggressive Patricks: We have no use for you here. Eviction feels scary, but for me, as long as I've given it enough thought first, I have never, ever regretted it.

—I disengage from conversations that treat dieting with reverence. Hard no. Absolutely not. Thank you, next. Fuck outta here with that.

i made you a shortcut!

—I try not to catastrophize.

This one is unfortunately not equally applicable to all people. If I'm on the fence about something, I think about the potential consequences of the action I'm considering taking. Will I die? If not—and the answer is usually not—and the potential benefit seems worth it, onward. This is easy for me to say because there are dangers others face that I do not. (There are also dangers I face that others do not.) So it's okay to exercise caution. I just hope that if you are stifled or limited, it's not because of self-imposed limitations but because of the situation *around* you. (That needs dismantling, too, and there are other books you can read about how to start doing that.) Sometimes I ask this question in the present tense— "Am I dying?"—like when I was out recently with friends at a bar and the chair I was sitting on broke. Twenty-seven-year-old me would have been mortified and probably cried and definitely left. She would have gone home and brutalized herself mentally. Today me did not. Was I ecstatic that a chair had broken beneath me, in front of friends and strangers? Not exactly. But I was also kind of fine. It got us loads of free shots and endless funnygirl fodder for the rest of the night, like how every so often I'd say to my friends, "Hey, guys, remember when I broke a chair?" And god bless Amy, who corrected me: "A chair broke," she said, meaning that the fault was with the furniture, not my incredibly powerful ass.

—I am straightforward.

I realized at some point that as self-conscious as I was about my body, I was even more self-conscious of seeming too self-conscious about it. I wanted more than anything to be *breezy*. But what is the prize for that? I went for a massage recently and in readying myself to give the speech said something I'd never said before: "I'm mentioning it because I'm self-conscious about it." Instead of the linguistic gymnastics I usually do—"I'm telling you for *your* benefit"—I was forthcoming about the fact that my speech was for *my* benefit. I hope there's a time when none of us has to give speeches, when nobody assumes anything about anybody's body, but until then, I will be vocal. I no longer consider trying to hide a worthy endeavor.

—I let myself be a complicated hypocrite.

For a long time, I viewed an idea reversal or inconsistency as a personal failure. Changing my mind about anything— meeting a friend for dinner, canvassing for a candidate three states away, going to yoga when I just want to lie in bed—was not only a disappointment but a betrayal (to friends, to democracy, to the universe). It was an impossible standard to live up to, and the only thing it guaranteed was my failure. I want to strive to be a kind person while also not turning my life into one long experiment in virtue signaling and betterment. I want to accept that I am not always good and sensitive, because no human is, instead of chastising myself when I fall short. Which reminds me:

—I try not to chastise myself.

Chastisement has felt like the most consistent action taken against me, or at least the one I am most sensitive to. At the heart of chastising is the insinuation that we are a disappointment. We could have done better. We *should* have done better. Nothing reduces me to tears quicker than being chastised, by my parents, by a boss, by a friend, by a stranger. Yell at me and I'll yell back. Be rude to me and fucking *stand* back. But chastise me and I crumble. So I do not do it to myself. (And I try not to let people do it to me.)

—I say no.

I say no to plans that don't interest me. I say no to people who want a slice of my time if I don't care for a slice of theirs, who I maybe once would have said yes to out of some delu-sional sense of owing it to them or wanting to score popularity points. (Here's what they never tell you about those: They are not redeemable. They are worthless.) Now I reserve my yeses for things I want to say yes to, and if my yes turns to a no by the time whatever thing comes around, I allow that, too. Decisions are not binding contracts, and I am allowed to reverse mine, even if other people find it annoying.

—I rest when I want to.

Not need to, *want* to.

—I get existential.

But in a good way! I think about how brief and uncertain our time on earth is and then I ask myself, "Is this worth worry-ing about?" Which doesn't mean I always answer no and also doesn't mean I never worry about how I look. It doesn't mean that real problems can't masquerade as superficial problems. It doesn't mean that invisible illnesses can't be life ruiners. It doesn't mean I don't give myself room to feel however I happen to feel whenever I'm feeling it. It just means that sometimes I ask myself (again—in a good way!) if, when I'm long gone, I will be glad that I spent so much time studying my jaw for signs of a double chin instead of reading a good book or talking to a friend. Or whether getting upset about an unflattering photo no one will ever see is a good use of my emotions. When I'm dead, I won't get to decide if people remember me as fat Carla or thin Carla, and mostly I hope they'll just remember me as funny Carla or kind Carla or author-of-that-book-they-really-liked Carla.

—I give myself the bad days.

Feeling Terrible World is a place I am allowed to visit because it is impossible to be a human and not feel bad about yourself sometimes. But I am only permitted on a day pass. I let myself take a spin on Mr. Toad's Wild Ride of Insecurity and It's a Small World and You Should Be Too, but then I make myself exit, no souvenirs allowed. If I am having trouble leaving, if I am hiding out after the gates close, I make myself tell a trusted friend. I fess up to my secret excursion. She then helps me manage my way down the now darkened path, streetlamps long extinguished, and gets me the fuck out of there.

—I try like hell to see myself as a whole person.

That magnetism I've talked about? Sometimes I've wondered if I'm memorable only because of how different I am, if strangers want to talk to me because I am an oddity. Or if I'm good at something, I'll find a way to reduce it to K-T and therefore not something to actually be proud of. For example, I can stand on my tiptoes in mountain pose for an extraordinarily long time. It's true that I was a pretty decent athlete as a kid, a yoga-goer for years, and I am a relatively strong person, but for some reason it's easy for me to tell myself, "It's just because your feet are so big and wide. You have an unfair advantage." You know who else has big feet? Michael Phelps. Commentators like to compare them to fins. He has an enormous wingspan. His body has given him an advantage in the pool. And yet, I don't think, *Sure, Michael Phelps is an amazing swimmer, but it's just because of the way his body is shaped,* because that would be psychotic. There are a lot of reasons he's an amazing swimmer, and though they include his DNA, they also include a lifetime of dedication and innate talent. In the end, it doesn't really matter why he's so good, it matters only that it's a joy to watch him in the pool. So I try to give that to myself when I'm hanging out in mountain pose like it's no big thing. Maybe my body does make it easier. But so what? Lucky me. (And if there's a competition for longest tippy-toe mountain pose that anybody knows about, please let me know.)

—But I'm not too rigid about trying to define what that whole is.

Because it's too hard and selfhood is too amorphous. The important things I know about myself haven't changed, ever: my compassion, my helpfulness, my humor, my humility. But the other stuff I may never have an answer for because there isn't one, and the answer doesn't much matter. Am I pretty or ugly? The answer's not important unless I make it important, in which case the only person whose opinion matters is mine.

—I honor my reactions, whatever they are.

I recently took a SoulCycle class, and afterward, a woman on a bike near mine said, "It doesn't bother the baby?" It took me a second to realize what she was asking: All those sprints and hill climbs and tap-backs—that was okay for the (nonexistent) child in my womb? I responded, "Ma'am, I am not pregnant." As her face went ashen and she fumbled to fix it, I said, "Don't worry—you didn't ruin my day, but maybe this is a good lesson for you in not commenting on people's bodies." A few weeks after that, a man boarded the elevator I was on, looked at me, and said, "Are you wearing a lot of layers?" I stared back at him but said nothing. I wasn't in the mood to educate. Sometimes I am and sometimes I'm not. Sometimes what I want to do is scream. Whatever I choose, whenever it happens, that is the right choice.

—I accept compassion.

Another massage, this one more recent. As I've gotten older, the list of things I need to mention has grown, so I don't always get to all of it. "These other scars," the massage therapist asked once I was on the table, because I hadn't mentioned them, "is that from another surgery?"

"The centipedes? Those are from liposuction," I said.

"Liposuction for . . ."

"Just to improve the appearance of my back," I told her. "There was no medical need for it or anything." And then, I don't know why, I kept going. "I had them between when I was eight and thirteen, so it's not like you have a say or anything when you're that age."

"Oh," she said. "You didn't ask to get them?"

"I did not."

"I'm really sorry," she said. *I'm really sorry.* Nobody had ever said that to me before.

"Thank you," I said. "I really appreciate that." And I meant it.

—I try not to value people's estimations of me unless those estimations are positive and not about my appearance.

There is one exception to my not caring what other people think of me, and that is anytime somebody shares something positive or complimentary about me that has nothing to do with my face or my body. The reason is that no one is harder on me than me. (I bet no one is harder on you than you.) I think a lot of the stories I've told in this book will be surprising to people who know me. People who have worked with me probably remember me as diligent and detail oriented and very much on my game. Acquaintances who have watched my life trajectory from afar probably see an impressive, slow ascendancy. The absentminded nervous wreck who has spent so much time feeling like a disappointment may look like a stranger to them. So when people are impressed by me, I try to give their opinions more credence than my own if my own opinion happens to be critical. Because I am impressive. And I have done well. And I have worked my ass off. (I have also been very, very lucky, because nobody succeeds without a fair amount of luck.) When people compliment my accomplishments or my confidence or my consistency or my work ethic, if my instinct is to bat them away, to explain all the reasons they shouldn't be impressed, to asterisk and append and refute, I stop myself. I remind myself that it is unlikely they are wrong and I am right. I remind myself that even though I have spent a lot of my life pretending, the chances that I could fool so many people are not high. And so instead I just say thank you.

—I go in the water every time.

By which I mean go in the water in a bathing suit. By which I mean I go in the water in *just* a bathing suit. There was a time after my proud Pitch Pine years, when I was a teenager in full bloom and eventually a self-conscious twenty- and thirty-something, when I felt I owed it to other people to cover up. Or maybe I just didn't trust them to behave if I didn't.

Once, on a friends trip to Las Vegas in my early thirties, I sat in the sweltering heat of a cabana dying to go swimming but put off by the gobs of people already in the pool. Many of them were drinking. Many of them looked exactly how one expects people in a Las Vegas pool to look, which is to say potentially menacing, at least to me. When I could no longer stand the heat, I walked to the pool with a towel pulled tight around me, dropped it in a puddle on the edge, and slunk as quickly as I could into the water, smooshing my back against the tiles so nobody was behind me. When I was sufficiently cooled, I waited for an opportunity that I knew would never come: when everybody would be facing the other direction, or when there'd be a sudden clearing of the waters that left the pool and deck suddenly empty. When I finally got myself out, it was because I was now freezing, the exact opposite as I'd been before. I found the nearest ladder, grabbed the now sopping-wet towel, wrapped it around myself, and scurried back to the cabana shivering and dripping.

These days I walk to the pool or ocean in my swimsuit—sometimes a bikini—and get in however is easiest and most comfortable for me. I get out the same way. If I offend anyone, I suppose they can avert their eyes, but that's not my concern. Occasionally I wonder, *What if someone says something? What if someone takes a picture? What if someone like the vampire is lurking on a chaise or there's a shark in the water? What if a photo of me in a swimsuit goes viral?* Remarkably, I then think, *That's not my concern, either.* Because even if that happens, I will not crumble. If I end up on some incel website as an object of aberration—something not unlikely in this time of intense scrutiny and cruelty, when ordinary people are attacked on social media all the time for having the audacity to exist—I won't love it, but I Will. Not. Fucking. Die. My sense of myself is set enough that although it wouldn't be pleasant to see an unwitting photo of myself taken by a troll, it would not break me.

There's that saying about attraction, how people are drawn to confidence and how you'll never find someone—or at least not the right someone—if you're not already comfortable with yourself. I never believed it, and I've never quite experienced it with dating, but it does feel like my body is less of a public spectacle now that I don't view it as one. Maybe it never was one as much as I thought. Or maybe it was and is, but I don't notice because I don't care, which is different from *pretending* not to care, and I know, because I pretended for a very long time. Now, on good days, which are most days, I truly do not care what other people—what *any* other people—think about my body. I do not care if somebody says something nasty or is inappropriately curious, and let's be honest, there are times I even like it, because it gives me a reason to unleash my inner bitch. I do not care if people think the outfit I'm wearing is unflattering or they wish I would cover up. I care only that my body is exalted, by me.

And so, I swim.

I always swim.

## Acknowledgments

This is a book I always wanted to write and tried so many times to write and often worried I would never write, so my first thank-you goes to anyone who ever encouraged me to keep going. Folks who attended a reading and asked, "When can I see more?" or told me to keep my chin up or just reminded me that writing is mostly thankless and we do it for ourselves, when it's important to us, for that reason alone, and we keep it up no matter what (maybe after a little nap). I shall pay it forward by reminding anyone writing anything that rejection is part of what we do and it feels horrible and I wish it didn't but oh well. If you are a writer, it's okay to let the bastards get you down but it'd be best if you could get up eventually (and it's fine to ask for help—just stick out your hand and ask someone to pull). As long as you believe in what you're doing, JUST KEEP GOING. There is only one choice in this Choose Your Own Adventure called writing.

So many people have given their time and energy and guidance for so long, in ways big and small, that they may not even remember now, but I do and always will. Those folks include Michelle Campbell, Heather Janoff Johnson and Krister Johnson, Randi Hecht and Glen Weiner, Eric Weiner, Megan Gilbert, Miranda Beverley-Whittemore, Alison Lowenstein, Bart Cameron, Jen Abramowitz, Lauren Iannotti, Edith Zimmerman, Jane Marie, JL Stermer, Alexis Berger, Dibs Baer, Jaime Harkin, Jo Piazza, Lane Zachary, Rick Reiken, Jay Baron Nicorvo, Teena Korman, Jane Friedman, and others I'm sure I am forgetting and will kick myself for leaving off this list.

All my gratitude and love goes to my perpetual cheerleading squad and chosen fam, whose encouragement has meant everything: Todd Shalom, Prana Topper, John DeCicco, Roy Chacko, Nicole Ovadia, Donna McWalters, Brad Loe, Olivia Loe, Meg Simione, Chad Flahive, Stephen Milioti, Stephanie Cutler Levin, Joy Fisher Williams, Meghan Mehlhop Berardi, Courtney Sinclair, Dylan Gadino.

Maura McWalters Chacko: You are a special kind of human. Your love and kindness and curiosity about this book (and about anything that anyone you love is doing) have meant more than you can possibly know, and I feel #blessed to have you in my corner. (I pity anyone who ends up *opposite* your corner.)

Melissa Sinclair: Kitten! Your persistent optimism and witchiness and "obviously you're going to publish your book"-ness were the light at the end of my sometimes pessimistic tunnel. I really did believe in myself because you believed in me. I can't thank you enough for your encouragement, and for being the person who makes me laugh until my stomach hurts (and then I pee). RIP, feel better.

Amy Gilkes Loe: Thank you for always making me know in my bones that it is my day to shine. Your love and generosity of spirit and time has meant everything, and I am so, so grateful not just to know you but to feel completely seen and understood. I know I am lucky enough to have someone by my side who is not only rooting for me but helping me get where I need to go. Your reads and notes made this book better (and have made countless other projects better too). If it's my day to shine, then it's your day to shine too.

My sister, Cara Sosenko Reilly, for her guidance and ear, and the rest of my family for their love, support, and general awesomeness: Michael, Lori, Steve, Matthew, Jacob, Hannah, Alexa, Ben, Brynn, Jenna, Cal, Aunt M, and Uncle A.

My parents, Elise and Alan Sosenko: Thank you for supporting me in more ways than I can name; for making my childhood one filled with theater and music and dance and culture and politics; for being supportive and interested and proud and wonderful, and for teaching me by example what it means to be kind and good and charitable. I know how lucky I got with you two, and I do not take that for granted. (Sorry about the title!)

The entire team at Dial Press—the place I know I was destined to land—whose enthusiasm and sense of community has felt like the perfect fit: Avideh Bashirrad, Marni Folkman, Corina Diez, Debbie Aroff, Donna Cheng, Aarushi Menon, Marlene Glazer, Allison King, Jennifer Rodriguez, Caroline Crouse, Sara Bereta: THANK YOU.

Alicia Hibbert, thank you so much for your insights and perspective.

Sharon Levy, for the illo of my dreams.

Talia Cieslinski, your sharp and incisive eye elevated this book again and again, and I am so glad to know you.

Annie Chagnot: This book would quite literally not exist

without you. You saw things in it (and me) that no one else did, and not only that, you gave of yourself long after it was required of you. I knew when this book ended up in your hands that it was safe and cared for. You have my deepest gratitude and always will.

Whitney Frick, thank you for your care, patience, guidance, reassurance, and dedication to making sure we got everything exactly right.

Lindsay Edgecombe: I don't even know where to begin. You are the level-headed, reassuring, steady, solid anchor to my frazzled, impulsive raw nerve. But you are not just an anchor, you are also whatever part of the boat does the steering (the wheel? I think you're the wheel. The extent of my boating knowledge ends with *Below Deck*). You are so stinkin' smart and regal and wonderful, and you put in so much work over such a long time to get this sold and be my advocate and really, really listen. You are the other person without whom this book would cease to exist.

Emma Caruso: EMMA. I've said it before and I'll say it again: You got more out of me than I knew I had to give. Your tireless work and willingness to push me (and/or push me back) made me a better writer and made this a better book. What could have been a weird situation ended up the best situation, and I could not have asked for a better partner on this project. You impressed me again and again, and I know my book ended up exactly where it was meant to.

My best girls, Scoutie and Loulou, who won't see this because they can't read.

Finally, thank you, fellow square pegs. We are the ones who make life interesting, and don't ever forget it.

## About the Author

CARLA SOSENKO is a journalist and author whose work has appeared in *The New York Times, Entertainment Weekly, Cosmopolitan, Marie Claire,* and other publications. She co-wrote TikToker Melissa Dilkes Pateras's book, *A Dirty Guide to a Clean Home.* Sosenko has undergraduate degrees in English and journalism from Boston University, and an MFA in creative writing from Emerson College. She lives in Brooklyn.

## *Books Driven by the Heart*

### Sign up for our newsletter and find more you'll love:

**thedialpress.com**

📷 @THEDIALPRESS

▶ @THEDIALPRESS